Thomas
Cook

PROVENCE
& THE CÔTE D'AZUR

BY
ROGER THOMAS

Produced by
Thomas Cook Publishing

Written by Roger Thomas
Updated by Nick Inman
Original photography by Adrian Baker
Original design by Laburnum Technologies Pvt Ltd

Editing and page layout by Cambridge Publishing
Management Ltd, Unit 2, Burr Elm Court,
Caldecote CB3 7NU
Series Editor: Karen Beaulah

Published by Thomas Cook Publishing
A division of Thomas Cook Tour Operations Ltd
Company Registration No. 1450464 England

PO Box 227,
The Thomas Cook Business Park,
Unit 18, Coningsby Road,
Peterborough PE3 8SB, United Kingdom.
E-mail: books@thomascook.com
www.thomascookpublishing.com
Tel: +44 (0)1733 416477

ISBN-13: 978-1-84157-704-3
ISBN-10: 1-84157-704-9

Text © 2006 Thomas Cook Publishing
Maps © 2006 Thomas Cook Publishing

First edition © 2004 Thomas Cook Publishing
Second edition © 2006 Thomas Cook Publishing

Project Editor: Diane Ashmore
Production/DTP Editor: Steven Collins

Although every care has been taken in compiling this publication, and the contents are
believed to be correct at the time of printing, Thomas Cook Tour Operations Ltd cannot
accept any responsibility for errors or omissions, however caused, or for changes in details
given in the guidebook, or for the consequences of any reliance on the information provided.

The opinions and assessments expressed in this book do not necessarily represent those of
Thomas Cook Tour Operations Ltd.

Printed and bound in Spain by: Grafo Industrias Graficas, Basauri.

Cover design by: Liz Lyons Design, Oxford.
Front cover credits: Left © Jean-Claude Dewolf/PhotoLibrary; centre © Chad Ehlers/Alamy;
right © Owen Franken/CORBIS
Back cover credits: Left © Franz-Marc Frei/CORBIS; right © Owen Franken/CORBIS

Contents

KEY TO MAPS

D994	Road number
619m ▲	Mountain
★	Start of walk/tour
🄸	Information
—	Ancient walls
☼	Viewpoint
✈	Airport
	Marshes

Introduction

Provence and the Côte d'Azur are undoubtedly the most alluring part of France and also perhaps the most complex. Although the historical heart of Provence was small, the area known as Provence today comprises the Côte d'Azur, part of the Alps and through to parts of Languedoc. Provence displays at least two incompatible personality traits. There is the pastoral face of Provence, a seductive visage of sleepy, golden-stoned farmhouses, sunflowers, lavender fields, vineyards, olive groves and improbably blue skies.

THOMAS COOK'S PROVENCE

In 1871 Thomas Cook advertised the new destinations of Menton, Nice, Toulon and Marseille as part of the 'Winter Arrangements' for that year. By the 1880s, Cook's Christmas and New Year trips to the South of France were very popular with his middle- and upper-class customers.

Clashing with this bucolic vision is the Provence of the coast, a cosmopolitan – and often chaotic – mix of glamorous resorts and dense development, a victory of style over simplicity, conspicuous consumption over quiet contemplation.

Further adding to the complex character of the area are its Alpine regions, where snowcapped peaks reach up into sunny skies; its high, empty plateaux, a no-man's-land between the Mediterranean and the Alps; its deep gorges like giant incisions in the earth's crust; its vast, lagoon-like flatlands along the Rhône delta; its retrospective qualities, embodied by an outstanding Roman heritage and idyllic medieval towns; and its dynamic, ever-onward economic impetus, driven by the high-tech Sun Belt industries of this blessed, beautiful, blighted 'California of Europe'.

Provence can give you whatever you want. A hundred kilometres from the coast, you can sit in a café in a fountained medieval square and watch the world go by – which will probably consist of one man and his bicycle or *madame* doing the shopping.

An hour's drive away, you can rub shoulders with the seriously rich and famous on a jewelled coastal strip that is still *the* place to go and be seen, that still has the cachet and that still attracts yachts worth more than the Gross Domestic Product of many Third World countries.

Provence

A scene of order and plenty: farmhouse and vineyard near Ménerbes in the Luberon

The land

Provence's boundaries embrace an amazing variety of scenery. Fertile valleys rise into rugged mountains, wooded hillsides and richly cultivated plains drift down to a palm-fringed, sandy coast. Towering crags and deep gorges in the Alpine country to the northeast contrast with the marshlands and long beaches of the Rhône delta to the southwest.

River and road

The fast-flowing Rhône has played a vital role in the development of trade. As well as defining Provence's western boundary, its broad valley is the region's crucial communications artery with the north, carrying the main road and rail links. Provence's other major river, the Durance, runs east to west, flowing into the Rhône south of Avignon.

Upland Provence

The mountain ranges striding across Provence are part of the geological upheaval that, over vast stretches of time, created the Alps. Mont Ventoux, the towering 1,909-m (6,263-ft) guardian of the northwestern approach to the region, has an overwhelming presence set off by vine-clad foothills. The northeastern gateway to Provence is through the

The Grand Cañon du Verdon, almost 1,000m (3,300ft) deep and an awe-inspiring sight

THE MISTRAL

The *mistral* has been known to drive man and beast mad. Suicide and murder rates are said to increase when this violent wind, which can reach speeds of 200kph (124mph), whistles down the Rhône Valley for anything from three to ten days. Its name derives from the Provençal *mistrau*, meaning master.

When pressure is high over the mountains or low over the sea, the wind sweeps down from the Massif Central to the Mediterranean, gaining in force as it funnels through the Rhône Valley. In summer, you will need a sweater even on the sunniest day. In winter, the chill factor seems positively Siberian – which is why all wise Provençals have windowless north-facing walls. Provence's decorative wrought-iron bell towers – known as *campaniles* – are another testament to the power of the *mistral:* the wind rushes harmlessly through the ironwork cage instead of toppling a conventional stone spire.

mountains of the Alpes-de-Haute-Provence, a highland area unremittingly Alpine in character.

South-central Provence also has its uplands. The Luberon Mountains, although only half the height of Ventoux, are nonetheless a prominent upland barrier between the Plateau de Vaucluse and the coast. Winter sunshine along the Riviera highlights the proximity of the snowy peaks of the Alpes-Maritimes, only a short distance inland. You are never far away from hills and mountains in Provence: even the flat Rhône delta suddenly rises into the craggy Alpilles, a western offshoot of the Luberon range.

Gorges and sunken valleys

The limestone rocks of this region result in weirdly eroded mountain features (the Vaucluse's Dentelles de Montmirail are a classic – see p35). The rock also produces a near-subterranean spectacle where the limestone massifs have been intercut with deep gorges by the patient action of rivers. The most spectacular is the Grand Cañon du Verdon (see pp128–9), where the river snakes between cliffs almost 1km (²/³ mile) high. Along the coast west of Marseille, limestone valleys have sunk into the sea to produce a strange, fjord-like shoreline of deeply indented inlets known as calanques (see p65).

Climate

Generally speaking, Provence is a region of hot, dry summers and mild, sunny winters: a climate that continues to entice the pleasure seekers as well as immigrants (usually from the grey northern latitudes) attracted as much by Provence's sunshine record as its new industries. An exception to this general rule can be made for the more northerly mountainous areas, which are cooler and wetter in spring and autumn but provide ideal conditions for winter sports. Western parts of Provence are regularly exposed to the mistral, a penetrating north wind (see box opposite). The hottest months are July and August, when temperatures soar to around 28°C (82°F) and rainfall is minimal. Some visitors prefer Provence in the spring, when the air is pleasantly warm and the countryside full of fresh, bright colours. Winters in the coastal region are mild, but autumn produces rain in October and November.

Economy

Despite massive tourism, agriculture remains an important part of the economy. Once-arid regions have long served as productive farmland thanks to centuries of irrigation, and Provence continues to produce more fruit and vegetables than any part of France. Honey, herbs and fields of lavender are much in evidence. Perfume, oils and soaps, textiles, crystallised fruit, mines and salt beds reflect some of the traditional Provençal occupations. There is a significant wine industry, based mainly on the Côtes du Rhône appellation. Much of Provence's industry is also concentrated in the Rhône Valley, and in recent years high-tech, scientific and communications industries have expanded considerably. The port of Marseille – one of the largest cities in France – is a busy commercial centre.

History

Mesolithic times (Middle Stone Age)	Earliest known inhabitants.	**4th–5th centuries AD**	Christianity gains in importance.
6000 BC	Evidence of Neolithic (New Stone Age) pottery and agriculture.	**471**	Arles invaded and taken by Visigoths, a western Germanic people.
Around 600 BC	Greek colonists found Massalia (Marseille).	**476**	The Roman Empire falls. Within 50 years, Provence is taken over by the Franks, another western Germanic people.
600–100 BC	Greeks settle along the coast, leading to clashes with the local population. Greeks enlist the aid of their Roman allies.	**736–739**	Saracens, nomadic Arabs from the deserts of Africa and the Middle East, invade southern France.
150–50 BC	Romans advance into Provence.	**768–814**	Charlemagne becomes king of the Franks and brings a semblance of order to Provence.
58–52 BC	Conquest of Gaul by Julius Caesar. Southern Gaul becomes Provincia – 'the Province'.	**855**	Provence is made a kingdom.
46 BC	Roman amphitheatre is built at Arles.	**9th century**	Continuing incursions by the Saracens.
19 BC	Construction of the Pont du Gard aqueduct near Nîmes.	**1032**	Provence becomes part of the Holy Roman Empire, though the Counts of Provence retain their independence.
1st century AD	Roman conquest of Provence completed early in the century.		
2nd–3rd centuries AD	Roman influence at its height: roads and new towns built.	**12th century**	The Crusades lead to increasing prosperity along the coast.

12th–14th centuries	The era of the troubadours, poet-musicians whose major theme was courtly love.
1274	The papacy is given land – known as the Comtat Venaissin – in Provence. This influential episode paves the way for further papal links.
1309	The French Pope Clement V escapes political interferences in faction-ridden Rome by setting up court in Avignon.
1378–1417	The Great Schism of the Church, with one pope in Rome and the other in Avignon.
1409	The University at Aix-en-Provence is established.
1434–80	Provence flourishes under the enlightened Count René of Anjou (Good King René).
c.1480	Provence becomes part of France.
1486	The union of Provence with the crown is ratified at Aix-en-Provence.

1539	The edict of Villers-Coterets declares French the official language of the region.
1545	Religious massacre in the Luberon Hills. Catholics and Protestants become embroiled in the Wars of Religion (1562–98).
1555	Nostradamus, physician, astrologer and citizen of Salon-de-Provence, publishes his predictions.
1580–95	Marseille becomes an important trading centre.
1720–22	The region is devastated by a terrible epidemic of the Plague, killing 100,000 in two years.
1789–99	The French Revolution. Provence remains largely anti-revolutionary. However, in 1792, 500 revolutionary volunteers from Marseille parade in Paris to the Song of the Rhine Army. The song is rechristened *La Marseillaise* and becomes the French national anthem.
1793	The Siege of Toulon, during which the young

	Napoléon Bonaparte makes his mark. Within a decade Napoléon crowns himself emperor and proceeds to conquer much of Europe.	**1939–45**	The Italians occupy Menton in 1940. Large-scale German occupation in 1942. Allied troops land on the Côte d'Azur in 1944. Germans remain in the mountains until 1945.
1814	Napoléon is forced by military defeat to abdicate and accept exile to the island of Elba.	**1945**	Col de Tende is ceded from Italy to France.
1815	Napoléon returns from exile and marches on Paris through eastern Provence in his short-lived 'Hundred Days' of power, but is defeated at the Battle of Waterloo. His second exile is on the island of St Helena.	**1962**	A new airport opens at Nice and soon becomes an international hub.
		1970	Autoroute opens between Paris and Marseille.
		1981	The high-speed TGV train links Paris with Marseille.
1860s	Casinos open at Monte-Carlo.	**1993**	The Grotte Cosquer discovered, revealing paintings and a culture that dates back over 25,000 years.
1914–18	World War I does not affect Provence territorially, though many of its men are killed in service.		
		1998	France hosts football's World Cup.
		2001	TGV service continued to St Raphaël and Nice.
		2003	Severe summer heatwave across France. Thousands of elderly people die.
		2004	Regional elections return a coalition of left-wing parties and ecologists to power.

Julius Caesar gazes down from a wall in Arles

Once a separate kingdom, Provence came under the French flag in 1486

Governance

Provence was once a kingdom on its own, though it officially became a part of France in 1486. Union with France did not have much influence on the way of life because of the great distances from Paris, reinforced by Provence's ancient ties with Italy. But everything was to change with the coming of the railways in the second half of the 19th century. Not only was the local Provençal language undermined by French, but the region attracted tourists and winter residents who created along the coast a cosmopolitan and wealthy society far removed in its values and lifestyle from the traditional countryfolk of the region.

It is this pattern that produced the extremes of right-wing power in the larger regional cities such as Nice and Cannes, and the contrasting socialist or communist strongholds inland. But even among the cities, there are exceptions to the rule.

The biggest city in Provence is Marseille. It has for many years been socialist (notwithstanding a worrying far-right enclave) with a suspicion of central government. Nice, on the other hand, has an unequivocally right-wing tradition. The city was ruled by a single family for many decades, and its reign ended only when charges of large-scale corruption were levied against the Mayor who, consequently, fled France to settle in South America.

When Algeria gained independence from France in the late 1950s, Provence became home for hundreds of thousands of *pieds noirs*, the French settlers who fled back to the mother country. Over the years these settlers have come to constitute a defined political force, and it seems probable that the presence of this uprooted community has accounted for the high level of support for the ultra-right-wing National Front in cities such as Toulon and Nice as well as in smaller places like Aubagne. Right-wing opinion is further fuelled by what is increasingly being perceived as a problem with North African immigrants and other 'foreigners'.

In the 1980s Jean-Marie Le Pen's National Front party started to gain a foothold in the south. Le Pen stood unsuccessfully as a candidate in Nice in the 1993 general election. His party saw a continuing rise in popularity during the 1990s but fell back after Le Pen was outvoted for France's presidency in 2002 by Jacques Chirac.

As a whole, Provence forms part of the Provence-Alpes-Côte d'Azur regional government, which is controlled by a left-wing coalition.

Culture

The culture of Provence finds expression everywhere: not just in artistic events, but in the way people live and in the traditions they have inherited from their forebears. In ancient times the region was a staging post between the Mediterranean in the south and Gaul to the north. The resulting cross-fertilisation of cultures has produced a unique mix.

Fruits of the earth at a village fête

Generalisation is a notorious activity. There will always be those who claim that the worldly inhabitants of Aix or Avignon harbour pretensions of sophistication unknown to the humble Provençal peasant (if such a species exists any longer). Nonetheless, it is reasonable to claim that Provençals are a proud and independent people who, though wary and to some degree suspicious of strangers, can be hospitable and generous to a fault once their trust has been earned. They have a dialectical language of their own, Provençal, which, although not commonly spoken today, is still taught as an option in most schools. It differs in many respects from classical French and is distinguished by the richness of its vowels (*see pp20–21*).

The people of Provence have a strong sense of their heritage and like to keep traditions alive

Festivals and fêtes

The pastoral tradition remains strong in Provence. The French in general have an almost mystical relationship with the land. Many city dwellers are today's representatives of families who, until relatively recently, lived a rural existence. Although the most modern of industries are nowadays to be found in Provence, the locals pride themselves on their deep attachment to the land. For them it is also a matter of continuity, seen in their reverence for traditions, many of which are rooted in rural antiquity.

Some of the festivals and *fêtes* with which the region abounds celebrate the harvesting of crops and the generosity of nature. Flower parades and wine festivals add zest and colour to the life of many a town and village; special events mark the custom of transhumance (the migration of sheep and cattle from winter plain to summer pasture), while fishermen's festivals are evidence of the importance of the sea. Adept though the early Christians were at giving new meaning to old customs, distinctly pagan undertones linger on in some of these local festivals.

Rural festivals flourish alongside more sophisticated occasions such as the Cannes Film Festival (*see pp96–7*) and musical events of various kinds. Sophisticates can enjoy everything from opera to jazz, for instance, at summer festivals in Arles and Avignon.

Architecture

Visitors with an eye for architecture will find much to delight them in Provence. The region's Roman remains are among the finest to be seen anywhere, and

Beehive-like *bories* near Gordes

richly decorated medieval churches demonstrate the degree of spiritual and material wealth the people have invested in their religious life. Romanesque chapels and wayside shrines add to the region's diversity. Among Provence's most distinctive features are the dry-stone beehive huts known as *bories*, originally the work of semi-nomadic shepherds; the best examples are in the Luberon.

Crafts old and new

The earliest inhabitants of Provence, although belonging to a hunting and fishing culture, were by no means savages. The necklaces of fishbone found on prehistoric skeletons uncovered here prove their manual dexterity and aesthetic sense.

Artistry of a different kind flourishes in Provence today, a region famous for the quality of its craftwork. From the religious figurines known as *santons* (*see p125*) to the blown-glass bubbles of Biot, Provence has a wealth of beautiful objects to tempt the discriminating visitor. It is not difficult to discern a continuity at work here, typified by the way old blends with new in this heritage-conscious part of France.

Festivals

Festivals and *fêtes* are a way of life in Provence. They range from small, informal village gatherings to prestigious international events, and embrace all aspects of life. They celebrate lavender and lemons, cinema and theatre, religion and the rice harvest, opera and jazz, wine and food.

Floats and parades mark many celebrations

The simple village festivals are great fun. Locals dress up in traditional costume, and there is usually an epic communal meal of many courses and different wines, which anyone can take part in for the price of an all-inclusive ticket. Ask at local tourist offices for details. Apart from the Cannes Film Festival, the main event of the year is Avignon's eclectic summer Festival of Dramatic Art. Aix-en-Provence's Festival of Art and Music is also particularly important.

The Gypsy Festival

On 24 and 25 May each year, gypsies from all over Europe make their pilgrimage to Stes-Maries-de-la-Mer, a custom that dates back at least to the 16th century. Their pilgrimage hinges on the figures of Sarah and the three Marys – Mary Magdalen, Mary Salomé (the mother of two Apostles) and Mary Jacobé (Jesus's aunt). According to legend, most of this group settled at Stes-Maries after arriving by boat from the Holy Land. The gypsies adopted the group's servant, Sarah, as their patron saint. On the 24th they carry a black statue of Sarah into the sea to be blessed along with the Camargue and its people, followed by the statues of Mary Salomé

and Mary Jacobé on the 25th.
In addition to its religious content, the festival is an animated, colourful occasion, with much music, spectacle and dance. A smaller pilgrimage, without the gypsies, takes place in late October.

January
Arles
International Gathering of Santonniers.
Tel: 04 90 18 41 20.
Bormes-les-Mimosas
Mimosalia Flower Show.
Tel: 04 94 01 38 38.

February
Menton
International Lemon Festival.
Tel: 04 92 41 76 76;
www.feteducitron.com
Nice
Carnival and Battle of Flowers.
Tel: 08 92 70 74 07;
www.nicecarnaval.com

April
Monaco
Monte-Carlo Spring Arts Festival (runs until May).
Tel: (337) 92 16 22 99.

May
Cannes
International Film Festival.
Tel: 04 92 99 84 22; www.cannes.fr
Stes-Maries-de-la-Mer
24–25 May: Gypsy pilgrimage.
Tel: 04 90 97 82 55.
Toulon
Festival of Music. *Tel: 04 94 18 53 00.*

June
La Ciotat
Festival of Cinema.
Tel: 04 42 08 61 32;
www.tourisme-laciotat.com
Tarascon
Tarasque Festival. *Tel: 04 90 91 03 52.*

July
Aix-en-Provence
Festival of Art and Music.
Festival of Dance. *Tel: 04 42 17 34 34.*
www.festival-aix.com
Antibes
Jazz Festival. *Tel: 04 92 90 50 00.*
Avignon
Festival of Dramatic Art (runs until
August and includes theatre, dance,
music, film and fringe events).
Tel: 04 90 27 66 50; www.festival-
avignon.com
Carpentras
Les Estivales (runs until August and
includes music, dance and theatre).
Tel: 04 90 63 00 78.
Hyères
Festival of Jazz. *Tel: 04 94 01 84 50.*
Manosque
Festival of Jazz. *Tel: 04 92 76 16 00.*
Orange
Chorégies d'Orange (festival of opera
and classical music). *Tel: 04 90 34 24 24.*

St-Rémy-de-Provence
Organa Festival (organ music).
Tel: 04 90 92 05 22.
Vaison-la-Romaine
Festival of Music, Theatre and Dance
(runs until August). *Tel: 04 90 36 02 11.*

August
Châteauneuf-du-Pape
First weekend in August: Fête de la
Véraison (marks the change in the
colour of the grape from green to red).
Tel: 04 90 83 71 08.
Malaucène
Summer Festival at the beginning of
August. *Tel: 04 90 65 22 59.*
Salon-de-Provence
Festival International de Musique.
Tel: 04 90 44 82 90.

September
Arles
Festival of the Rice Harvest.
Tel: 04 90 18 41 20.
Cassis
Festival of Wine. *Tel: 04 42 01 71 17.*

December
Marseille
Santons Fair (runs until January).
Tel: 04 91 13 89 00.

Carnival parade in Nice

Impressions

Provence is a fairly complicated jigsaw puzzle. At the risk of stating the obvious, the basic advice for the first-time visitor is to do one of two things: head inland for the escapist rural retreat (found anywhere within 50km (31 miles) of the coast) or pack the swimsuits and the evening dress for the beaches and casinos. Some prefer the lush vineyards of the Vaucluse, others the more barren high country of the Var or the mountains of the Alpes-de-Haute-Provence. The glamour and glitz of Cannes and St-Tropez cast an irresistible spell over many, while others prefer the uncomplicated appeal of family resorts such as La Ciotat or the natural wonders of the Camargue.

Finding your way around

This book is subdivided into the region's five *départements* – Vaucluse, Bouches-du-Rhône, Var, Alpes-Maritimes and Alpes-de-Haute-Provence. If each *département* were a self-contained entity with its own unique, distinct set of scenic characteristics, then the task of explaining 'what is where' in Provence would be a simple one. But Provence is not that tidily arranged. The classic violator of departmental borders is the Côte d'Azur, the 'azure-blue coastline'. We have all heard of it, but where exactly is it? Theoretically it stretches

from St-Raphaël (in the Var), along the coast of the Alpes-Maritimes, through the independent Principality of Monaco to the Italian border. In practice, the Côte d'Azur label is often applied to the entire French Riviera as far west as Cassis (in the Bouches-du-Rhône).

Similarly, major landscape features such as the Montagne du Luberon and the Alpine Parc National du Mercantour span departmental boundaries. Overlap also applies to the precise definition of Provence itself. Within the context of this book, Nîmes, Pont du Gard and the western

PERCHED VILLAGES OF PROVENCE

'A village stands on high ground, partly as a defence against the Saracens, but mainly for the good view . . . The peasants, who know how to enjoy life, take time to look at things.' These were the words of Provençal writer Jean Giono (1895–1970).

The 'perched villages' (*villages perchés*) of Provence were built for security in troubled medieval times. Built in dense clusters that took maximum advantage of steep slopes and heights, the villages almost merge into their surroundings. However, very few proved to be impregnable.

By the start of this century many were in a sorry state, the locals understandably preferring life in newer houses with running water and other conveniences.

Today the immaculately renovated villages – many with shops, artisans' quarters and exclusive restaurants – make every attempt to attract rather than repel visitors.

Camargue are all included within the Bouches-du-Rhône section, even though this is not strictly correct (these places are in the *département* of the Gard).

Cities and coastal resorts

Provence, for all its natural beauty, also boasts big cities and busy resorts. The cities vary from stylish Aix to sprawling Marseille, slightly dowdy Arles to self-confident Avignon. The resorts, too, have distinct characters. A coastal strip that seems on first impressions to be a continuous, unbroken development reveals undeniable differences on closer examination.

The old maxim 'Cannes is for living, Monte-Carlo for gambling and Menton for dying' still has a ring of truth. Nice and St-Tropez, the other really famous places along the coast, have similarly strong – and surprising – personalities: surprising because of the vastness of Nice (which is more city than resort) and the smallness of world-famous St-Tropez.

Resorts such as Hyères and Ste-Maxime manage to preserve a sense of dignity on an intensely developed, over-exploited coast, which unfortunately shows all the signs of overheating (in the non-climatic sense). Yet there are still areas of relative wilderness: the indented coast between Marseille and Cassis, the lovely Îles d'Hyères and, to a lesser extent, the mountain-backed shorelines fringing the Massif des Maures and Massif de l'Esterel.

Villefranche-sur-Mer, one of the less frenetic resorts on the popular Côte d'Azur

Traditional Provençal women 'cowboys'

In the country

Provence's landscapes range from sunny valleys to snowy peaks. The characteristic Provençal scene – the golden-stoned farmhouse set amongst sun-baked vineyards – is most readily found in the Vaucluse or Bouches-du-Rhône. The higher country of the Vaucluse Plateau and the Var offers huge, open spaces that reveal a hint of Alpine influence. The Alps themselves lie further north and east, in the thinly populated upper reaches of the Alpes-de-Haute-Provence and the Alpes-Maritimes.

Customs and lifestyle

Provence is a land where undue haste is not considered a virtue. Its people are far from indolent, but they instinctively believe that quality of life is much more important than intensity of activity. Even in the busiest cities such as Marseille, time is found for a leisurely lunch.

To understand the character of the Provençals, one must appreciate that from time immemorial their lives have been shaped by the slow turn of the seasons. They are essentially a rural people with respect for the land, and this respect applies even to city folk, whose gardens are often small islands of perfection. Their natural reserve quickly gives way to open-handed generosity when they feel you are to be trusted, and their laughter and high spirits are infectious.

A hint of formality

The sense of being part of an old civilisation where the values of yesteryear are not easily discarded is confirmed by the etiquette of the region. Women are still greeted in the customary way with two or three kisses on the cheek (amongst men, even close friends observe a quick handshake), but this does not imply any taking of liberties. Manners tend to be far more formal than in Britain, for example, and the tourist would be well advised to address people as *monsieur, madame* or *mademoiselle*.

It also pays to know a little French, for an attempt to speak the language, however imperfectly, is regarded as an act of courtesy to the host country. Remember, too, that people living in the Provençal countryside are much more conservative than city dwellers in their attitude to dress. Topless bathing is perfectly acceptable on the beaches, but walking around town in beachwear is not. It is also a breach of propriety to enter a church or cathedral while scantily dressed.

Traditional costume

Tradition plays a large part in the life of Provence. The traditional costumes

worn by many families during the numerous festivals bring a distinctive feel to life in the region. Christmas and Easter have their own special rituals, which are still faithfully observed.

In day-to-day matters, too, old customs die hard. Shopping is less a chore than a social activity that gives savour to life. Open-air markets not only offer goods and produce of all kinds, they also bring a town or village together once a week. These markets serve as a natural interface between locals and visitors to the region. To

Fête de la Sainte Eloi, Chateaurenard

> ### Opening times
> Most religious sites are open at all reasonable times, though sightseeing visits should always take place when church services are not being held. Other sites often close in winter or have very restricted opening hours. Even in summer, many (especially museums) are closed at some time during the week, normally on Monday or Tuesday. Specific details are given for each site mentioned; in general, all main sites are freely accessible and open daily during the tourist season.

outsiders, they reveal how carefully the Provençals select the items that make up their everyday meals. These are folk not easily fobbed off with anything less than the best, for it seems that nature has equipped them with antennae highly sensitive to the shoddy and second-rate, enabling them to maintain high standards in a rapidly changing world.

A social dimension to food

Food, of course, is more than mere sustenance to the Provençals. Their insistence on quality reflects an attitude to food – found throughout France, in fact – that has profound social, even artistic, dimensions.

Calorie-conscious tourists may view such delights with trepidation, deciding perhaps that some of the salads served as separate courses are meals in themselves. What they should not deny themselves is the experience, for in Provence meals are social occasions to be enjoyed to the full.

Café society also flourishes here, and not only among the wealthier classes. Enjoying a *pastis* or *café crème* after a wander round the market is something that practically everyone does on a regular basis. It is part of the unhurried *vie provençale* (Provençal way of life).

Language

Provençals are justly proud of the fact that their dialectical language continues to exist despite all the pressures exerted by mass communications and the cultural dominance of French. The official language of the region is, of course, French, but Provençal – the tongue of the medieval troubadours – still survives. Not that you are likely to hear it being spoken in the streets. Provençal today lives on as a literary language studied at school or university, and also – more visibly – on bilingual place-name signs.

Provençal is derived from the vulgar Latin that entered the region with Roman colonisation. It is a dialect of the southern Languedoc (the *langue d'oc* as opposed to the *langue d'oïl* of northern France, *oc* and *oïl* meaning 'yes' in the south and north respectively). Its written form reaches back ten centuries, for around the year 1000 Provençal became the language of courtly poetry. Although gradually

Provençal is still very much in evidence on road signs

Arlesiennes decked out in traditional finery

superseded by French as a written language, it survived as a spoken tongue until relatively recent times.

Provençal differs from French in the openness of its vowels. In standard French, unstressed vowels tend to contract or to disappear altogether, but in Provençal they are distinctly voiced. This makes for a rounder, more musical language, which in many respects is closely related to Catalan.

Optional lessons

A new awareness of the language arose in the first half of the 19th century, when the poet Frédéric Mistral helped found the Félibrige movement, which aimed to restore the Provençal language and codify its spellings. But revival proved a forlorn hope, and by the time Mistral received the Nobel Prize in 1904, Provençal had already given way to French as the tongue in everyday use.

Today the language is taught as an option in most schools, and there is a faculty in the Provençal language and literature at the University of Aix-en-Provence. Its official encouragement should ensure its survival. It would take a brave – or foolhardy – person today to echo the sentiments of 19th-century tourist Lady Hester Stanhope who, in 1846, dared to pronounce it 'a most disagreeable jargon'!

Vaucluse

Vineyards, lavender fields and craggy hills cover this *département*, a beautiful area that lies under the watchful gaze of Mont Ventoux. The Vaucluse's western boundary is defined by the wide valley of the Rhône. Eastwards, the rich Côtes-du-Rhône vineyards rise into a roller-coaster landscape of green hills and valleys spread beneath the bare-topped heights of Mont Ventoux.

Rows of lavender bushes are a common sight

Apt

This town, which spreads itself out across a wide valley on the northern approach to the Luberon Mountains, is more noteworthy for its location than its inherent charm. It is, however, well known for its associations with a number of edible things. Foremost amongst these are speciality chocolates and candied fruit.

Apt is synonymous with sweets. There are a number of manufacturers, some of whom specialise in glacéed or crystallised fruits – cherries, plums, pears, apricots, pineapples, etc. These and many more mouthwatering confections are on sale at the Saturday market, along with a magnificent array of local produce. The market, in the rue des Marchands, is a social as well as a shopping experience. Cars are banned from the town centre to make way for stallholders, musicians, jugglers and craftspeople. Apt also has another, smaller 'farmers' market' on Tuesday morning (April to December) at cours Lauze de Perret.

Although the approach to the town is shabby and undistinguished, there are many interesting and attractive little corners to explore. But most visitors inevitably look further afield, for the town is an excellent base for exploring the **Parc Naturel Régional du Luberon** (*see pp24–5*).

Ancienne Cathédrale Ste-Anne

This 11th-century building in the centre of town, dedicated to the mother of the Virgin Mary, also shows evidence of an earlier religious settlement in its two ancient crypts (Romanesque and pre-Romanesque).

Fountain in Apt; the town was once a place of pilgrimage but is now associated with sweets

Vaucluse

Maison du Parc Naturel Régional du Luberon (Luberon Regional Natural Park Office)

The visitor centre, in an attractive 17th-century mansion, has a wide range of information on the park, including a palaeontology museum.

1 place Jean-Jaurès. Tel: 04 90 04 42 00. Open: daily 8.30am–noon & 1.30–7pm (6pm in winter). Closed: Sat & Sun in winter. Admission charge.

Musée d'Histoire et d'Archéologique

Exhibits cover prehistory, the Gallo-Roman period (Apt was a prosperous Roman colony), and ceramics from the 17th to 19th centuries.

Rue de l'Amphithéâtre.
Tel: 04 90 74 95 30. Open: by appointment only for group guided tours.
Admission charge.

Ste-Anne's cathedral, Apt

Tour: the Luberon

The Parc Naturel Régional du Luberon, established in 1977, stretches for over 60km (37 miles) between Cavaillon in the west and Manosque in the east, taking in two *départements* – the Vaucluse and Alpes-de-Haute-Provence (*see p137* for details). This tour concentrates on the western part of the park – an area dominated by the uplands of the Petit (Small) Luberon, which rise to 700m (2,297ft) – and the picturesque villages that are often perched high on the slopes.

The tour, which at a leisurely pace could take all day, begins at Apt, the region's major town and location of the visitor centre for the park (see p23).

Take the D48 southeast to the perched village of Saignon and its Romanesque church. The D232 and D113 lead south to Buoux and the Fort de Buoux.

1 Fort de Buoux

This is an abandoned fortified village standing high on a natural platform and accessible by foot and full of interest. The bastions, ramparts, keep, rock dwellings, 13th-century church and remains of a recently excavated medieval village can all be seen.

Follow the D943 south through the Combe de Lourmarin, the only road to cut through the Luberon Mountains for 20km (12 miles) on either side, to Lourmarin.

2 Lourmarin

Writers Henri Bosco (who described the Luberon Mountains as a 'blue whale') and Albert Camus, who won the Nobel prize for literature in 1957, both lived in this attractive village, which is guarded by a Renaissance château (guided tours available, tel: 04 90 68 15 23). From here you can take a short detour further south to visit the Abbaye de Silvacane (*see p49*).

From Lourmarin, return along the D943, turning left along the D36 to Bonnieux.

3 Bonnieux

The Provence of Peter Mayle, undoubtedly the Luberon's best-known contemporary English writer, is populated by simple – and not so simple – country folk.

This bucolic picture is not, of course, wholly accurate. Bonnieux, Lacoste and **Ménerbes**, which are all featured in his books, are fashionable places that combine sophistication with a certain down-to-earth charm. Bonnieux is a lively, attractive, terraced village situated on a steep hill commanding wonderful views across to Lacoste, Gordes, the Vaucluse Plateau and Mont Ventoux. Its unusual **Musée de la Boulangerie** (Museum of Baking, *tel: 04 90 75 88 34, open Wed–Mon 10am–12.30pm & 2.30–6pm, admission charge*), converted from an ancient bakery, is worth a visit.

Take the D3/D109 to Lacoste.

4 Lacoste

Lacoste is famous – or infamous – for its château, home of Donatien Alphonse François, better known as the Marquis de Sade (1740–1814). Take the D109 to Ménerbes, which passes the **Ancienne Abbaye St-Hilaire**, a 12th-century religious site with a surviving chapel. Ménerbes was the scene of a long siege in the 16th-century Wars of Religion, when it was a Protestant stronghold. Its ancient fortifications are now largely in ruins.

From Ménerbes take the D188 to Oppède-le-Vieux.

5 Oppède-le-Vieux

Oppède towers over a wild landscape of rocks and woodland. Another perched village with a past dominated by conflict, it was abandoned at the end of the last century. It has since been rediscovered by artists and intellectuals, who have sympathetically restored its old houses and given the village a new role as an arts and cultural centre.

The D176 leads to the small village of Maubec and onwards to the D2. Cross the N100, staying on the D2 for Gordes (see pp36–7). Continue east on the D2, turning right on the D102 for Roussillon (see p40). Return to Apt via the D4/N100.

Avignon

The historic, stylish city of Avignon stands alongside the curving Rhône on a wide, flat valley. It is the largest and most important city in the Vaucluse. Visitors approaching the city might begin to suspect that Avignon does not live up to expectations. Fear not: the historic heart of the city will not disappoint. Persevere through the bland suburbs to the ring of city walls, still complete, that encloses the Avignon of the guidebooks.

Looking up to a tower of the Palais des Papes

The walls, still defended by 39 towers, date from medieval times. Avignon's history can be traced as far back as the Bronze Age, though it was in the 14th century that it became the city of the Popes. In 1309 Pope Clement V sought refuge here from the factionalism of Rome, establishing an administrative base that eventually rivalled the Vatican. The glory of the imperial Palais des Papes (Palace of the Popes) confirms Avignon's medieval status.

Carved doors, church of St Pierre, Avignon

The city is today a major artistic centre with a prestigious summer festival, focused largely on theatre and film. Across the river stands Avignon's sister city, **Villeneuve-lès-Avignon**.

Cathédrale Notre-Dame-des-Doms
This 12th-century Romanesque church holds the tombs of two pontiffs.
Place du Palais. Tel: 04 90 86 81 01.
Open: daily 8am–6pm.

Musée Calvet
A fine 18th-century mansion that contains classical and modern paintings, wrought-iron pieces, Greek sculpture and exhibits of local prehistory bequeathed by Dr Esprit Calvet to his native town.
65 rue Joseph Vernet. Tel: 04 90 86 33 84.
Open: Wed–Sun, 10am–1pm & 2–6pm.
Admission charge (free in winter).

Musée du Petit Palais
The museum, based at the episcopal palace acquired by the papacy in 1335, contains a huge collection of paintings and sculptures, mostly Italian, from the 13th to 15th centuries.

*Place du Palais. Tel: 04 90 86 44 58.
Open: summer, Wed–Mon, 10am–1pm &
2–6pm; winter, Wed–Mon, 9.30am–1pm
& 2–5.30pm. Admission charge.*

Musée Requien

Dedicated to Esprit Requien
(1788–1851), the great Avignon
naturalist, the museum has collections
based on local botany, zoology and
geology, a natural history library and a
herbarium with over 200,000
specimens.
*67 rue Joseph Vernet, next to the Musée
Calvet. Tel: 04 90 82 43 51. Open: Mon &
Wed–Sat, 9am–noon & 2–6pm. Free
admission.*

Palais des Papes

This majestic papal palace, with its
dominant, soaring architecture, was
built in the 14th century as a fortress-
cum-palace to serve as a French base for
the popes. Its battlements and towers,
reaching to 50m (164ft), are impressive.
Within the walls, the overpowering
dimensions are even more evident –
especially the 48-m (157-ft) long Grand
Tinel (Banqueting Hall) and Grande
Audience (Great Audience Chamber).
The palace is an overlap of two styles,
reflecting the personalities of two popes,
Benoit XII and Clement VI. The first
palace is sober, even austere, whereas the
second is an opulent homage to an all-
powerful prelate. During the French
Revolution the Palais was ransacked and
first turned into a prison, then a
barracks, which it remained until the
early 20th century.
*Place du Palais. Tel: 04 90 27 50 00.
Open: Oct–Feb, daily, 9.30am–5.45pm;*
*Mar–June, daily, 9am–7pm; July, daily,
9am–9pm; Aug–Sept, daily, 9am– 8pm.
Admission charge.*

Pont St-Bénézet

This famous landmark is celebrated by
the ubiquitous folk song *Sur le pont
d'Avignon.* (The dancing took place on
an island in midstream, so technically
the wording should be '*sous* (under) *le
pont*' not '*sur* (on) *le pont*'.) The bridge
itself comes as something of an
anticlimax, for it no longer crosses the
river. The stunted structure, once 900m
(2,953ft) long, was largely washed away
in a 17th-century flood. Nevertheless, a
walk along what is left of the narrow
bridge is a ritual for all visitors to
Avignon.
*Tel: 04 90 85 60 16. Open: as for Palais
des Papes. Admission charge.*

A *trompe l'oeil* painting at Palais du Roure

Walk: Avignon

Although it is a large city, Avignon's main places of interest are easily visited on foot, for they are contained within a compact area defined by a ring of walls running continuously for 5km (3 miles) around the city centre. If you are arriving by car, use one of the car parks located alongside the walls. Pedestrianised shopping streets lead off from the rue de la République, the main thoroughfare through the heart of the walled town.

Allow at least half a day for the walk, with extra time for a full visit to the Palais des Papes.

From the Office de Tourisme at 41 cours Jean-Jaurès (tel: 04 32 74 32 74) walk along rue Joseph Vernet.

1 Rue Joseph Vernet

This street is one of the most elegant in Avignon, along which you will pass restaurants and expensive shops selling *haute couture* and high-class confectionery. The Musée Calvet and the Musée Requien are located side by side on the street.

Continue along rue Joseph Vernet towards place Crillon.

2 Place Crillon

Place Crillon's furniture shops sell exclusive antique and modern pieces. Porte de l'Oulle, a gateway in the town walls, leads to the main road bridge over the Rhône.

At the far end of rue Joseph-Vernet, turn right, then first right into rue Petite Fusterie (the antique dealers' quarter), then turn left into rue St-Agricol.

3 Église St-Agricol

Église St-Agricol is located along the street of the same name. Dating from the 14th to 16th centuries, it is dedicated to Avignon's patron saint. It is one of the city's best Gothic edifices, with a beautifully carved 15th-century façade and fine medieval works of art.

Continue on to the Palais du Roure on rue Collège du Roure at the bottom of the place de l'Horloge.

4 Palais du Roure

The 15th-century Palais du Roure houses a cultural centre for Provençal studies and a museum of popular art and traditions (open to the public Tue at 3pm, or on request, *tel: 04 90 80 80 88*). Avignon's café society congregates along the place de l'Horloge, a wide, open space full of brasseries and flanked by the City Hall and Opera House.

Rue Villar leads to an even more impressive open space, the place du Palais at the foot of the mighty Palais des Papes (Palace of the Popes) and Cathédrale

Notre-Dame-des-Doms. At the far end of the square is the Musée du Petit Palais. From here, little alleyways lead to the famous pont St-Bénézet (signposted). From the bridge, walk alongside the ramparts to the flights of steps that zigzag up the cliff face to the beautiful gardens of Rocher des Doms.

5 Jardins Rocher des Doms

These restful gardens, set on a high outcrop overlooking Avignon and neighbouring Villeneuve-lès-Avignon, command wonderful views northwards across the majestic Rhône. This is the perfect place for a picnic, with play areas, an ornamental lake and shady pathways.
Take the Escaliers Ste-Anne (the steps down from the gardens) to rue Banasterie.

6 Chapelle des Pénitents Noirs

At this point, you can take a short detour northwards along rue Banasterie for the Chapelle des Pénitents Noirs, an 18th-century baroque edifice. Southbound, rue Banasterie leads to place St-Pierre and its church (14th to 16th centuries), noted for its flamboyant Gothic-style façade and huge carved walnut doors. Follow rue des Fourbisseurs to place St-Didier, which, like place St-Pierre, has a fine Renaissance church.
Rue Laboureur and rue Frédéric-Mistral lead to rue de la République and the Musée Lapidaire, which contains archaeological finds from the Egyptian, Greek and Gallo-Roman periods. Tel: 04 90 85 75 38. Open: Wed–Sun 10am–1pm, 2–6pm. Admission charge.

The popes

Provence played a notable part in the convoluted religious life of the Middle Ages when, in the 14th century, it became the seat of the papacy. This curious chapter in the history of Provence began in 1309 with the decision of Pope Clement V, who was French by birth, to set up court in a Dominican monastery in Avignon (he had never actually reached Rome since his election in 1305). He thus began what was unflatteringly described as 'the second Babylonian captivity of the Church', a period of preoccupation with power, legalism and money-raising.

The popes who followed his lead were a mixed bunch: Urban V was later beatified, but Benoit XII was regarded as uncharitable and avaricious, and Clement VI – of noble birth and with tastes to match – continued his love affair, ennobled his 'nephew' and built a sumptuous 'new' palace reflecting his enthusiasm for the arts and high living. He also bought the city of Avignon (in return for absolution for the owner's sin of complicity in the murder of her first husband) for 80,000 florins, a sum only five times the cost of his inaugural banquet.

The Great Schism

In 1377 Pope Gregory XI, a Frenchman, was persuaded to move the Holy See back to Rome and try to restore order to the warring states. But the Italian Urban VI, who soon followed him in 1378, upset the cardinals of France so much that they left Rome and elected a new French pope in his place, Clement VII, recognised by the King of France. Thus was born the

Great Schism of 1378–1417, with one pope in Rome and another in France. Christendom was split in two, both geographically and politically, with the 'Clementines' drawn up against the 'Urbanists' They excommunicated each other and issued bulls calling for crusades against each other. The death of one or other of the popes gave rise to fresh elections.

The two papacies were joined by a third in 1409, created by cardinals of the two parties hoping to find a compromise. Finally the crisis was resolved through a Church Council, at which a new pope was elected following the abdication or deposition of the other three.

Meanwhile, Avignon appears to have become exhausted by the controversy long before the Schism was resolved, for in 1403 the last of the Antipopes, Benoit XIII, was smuggled out of the Palais by a secret passage after a five-year siege by French troops, and the city settled into a more tranquil life.

Even after the Schism, however, Avignon was governed by a succession of papal legates. It remained papal property until the French Revolution.

Facing page above: Pope Clement V, who made Avignon the seat of the papacy
Left and above: the Avignon papal palace is a symbol of worldly wealth

Beaumes-de-Venise

This large village is known to many
through its famous Muscat de Beaumes-
de-Venise, a distinctive sweet amber-
coloured wine. The village stands at the
southern approach to the rugged
Dentelles de Montmirail (*see p35*), about
10km (6 miles) north of Carpentras.
Narrow terraced streets climb into the
hillside from an attractive central square
lined with cafés and shops.

One kilometre to the west is the
Chapelle de Notre-Dame d'Aubune,
dating from the 9th and 10th centuries
and topped by a Romanesque bell tower.
Frankish and Saracen forces are said to
have clashed here in the 8th century.

Wine-lovers will need no introduction
to the villages around Beaumes –
Vacqueyras, Gigondas, Sablet, Rasteau,
Cairanne – for this area on the flattish
eastern flank of the Rhône Valley
produces the premier Côtes-du-Rhône
Villages, a robust, peppery red wine of
formidable strength.
*Beaumes is 9km (5¹/₂ miles) north of
Carpentras.*

Bédoin

In winter, Bédoin is a sleepy village. In
summer, it is transformed into a busy
holiday centre. Do not try to drive
through Bédoin on Monday morning,
when the main street becomes a
marketplace packed with stallholders
and milling crowds.

Bédoin's popularity rests on its
location. It stands at an altitude of over
300m (984ft), surrounded by beautiful
wooded hills on the southern slopes of
Mont Ventoux. Campsites and holiday
homes attract a cosmopolitan mix of

St-Siffrein's cathedral at Carpentras

visitors (the area is particularly popular
with the Dutch). You can soak up the
sunny atmosphere in one of the many
cafés along Bédoin's long main street.

For the children, the village has an
excellent municipal swimming pool.
Historically, there is little evidence of
Bédoin's ancient roots (it was founded
in the 8th century), though there are
vestiges of the medieval ramparts in the
streets leading up to the hilltop church.
*Bédoin is 15km (9 miles) northeast of
Carpentras.*

Carpentras

For visitors, interest in Carpentras lies
within the historic heart of the town;
this is encircled by a ring of main
arteries that follows the line of medieval
fortifications (demolished in the 19th
century). Compact central Carpentras is
easily explored on foot. The towering
Porte d'Orange, the main gateway into
the old town from the north, is a lone,
splendid medieval survivor. From this
14th-century gateway, the rue d'Orange

and rue de l'Evêché lead into the pedestrianised town centre, dominated by the **Palais de Justice** (Law Courts) and the **Cathédrale St-Siffrein**. Guided tours of the Palais de Justice – formerly the episcopal palace, dating from the 17th century – are available in summer (enquire at the Office de Tourisme, 170 allée Jean-Jaurès). The cathedral, which is of limited interest, was started in 1404 and completed in the 17th century.

It is worth searching for the **Arc de Triomphe** hidden behind the Palais de Justice. This beautifully decorated Roman arch was probably built at about the same time as the more famous monument at Orange (*see p38*).

One of the Vaucluse's main markets is held in Carpentras each Friday morning. Look out for the stalls selling *berlingots*, the special caramel sweets for which the town is famous.

Musée Comtadin-Duplessis

Downstairs, the Musée Comtadin contains a wide-ranging collection of regional artefacts, including weapons, *santons* and bells worn by cattle and sheep. The Musée Duplessis, upstairs, displays the work of 18th-century Carpentras painter Joseph-Siffrein Duplessis and others.

234 boulevard Albert-Durand.
Tel: 04 90 63 04 92. Open: Apr–Sept, Wed–Mon, 10am–noon & 2–7pm; Oct–Mar till 4pm. Admission charge.

Synagogue

The oldest synagogue in France, this ancient building dates from the 14th century when Jews were banished from the Kingdom of France but were granted refuge in Carpentras by Pope Clement V. There is still a considerable Jewish community living in the area.

Place Maurice Charretier.
Tel: 04 90 63 27 15. Open: Mon–Thur 10am–noon & 3–5pm, Fri till 4pm. Closed: on Jewish holidays. Free admission.
Carpentras is 26km (16 miles) northeast of Avignon.

Mont Ventoux provides the backdrop to the beautifully situated village of Bédoin

Châteauneuf-du-Pape, a place synonymous with fine wines

Cavaillon

Fruit and vegetable fields fill the flattish, well-irrigated countryside around Cavaillon. One product in particular – the melon – is the mainstay of the area's thriving market gardening economy. Unsurprisingly, the town is home to the second-largest wholesale fruit and vegetable market in France.

For a panoramic view of the fertile Cavaillon Plain, Mont Ventoux, the hills of the Luberon and the Alpilles, follow the path that climbs Colline St-Jacques from the Roman Arch (re-erected here in 1880) at place François-Tourel. On the hill you will find the 12th-century **Chapelle St-Jacques**, on the site of a temple to Jupiter. Cavaillon's main historic monument is the Cathédrale St-Véran, though the town also contains a richly decorated synagogue and small museum. The latter reflect the town's long-standing links with the Jewish religion, for Cavaillon was one of four Jewish centres – along with Avignon, Carpentras and L'Isle-sur-la-Sorgue – in the Comtat Venaissin, the land given to the papacy by France in 1274.

Cathédrale St-Véran

This Romanesque cathedral dates from the end of the 12th century. It was built in the same elegant style as Avignon's Cathédrale Notre-Dame-des-Doms. *Along place Voltaire.*

Musées Archéologique et Patrimoine de Cavaillon

Housed in the old hospital chapel, the museum is devoted to local prehistory and the Gallo-Roman period. Exhibits include preserved Gaulish food. *At the intersection of Grand Rue and cours Gambetta. Tel: 04 90 76 00 34. Open: summer, Wed–Sun, 9.30am–12.30pm & 2.30–6.30pm; Oct, Wed–Sun, 9am–noon & 2–5pm; winter by appointment only. Admission charge.*

Cavaillon is 24km (15 miles) southeast of Avignon.

Châteauneuf-du-Pape

Châteauneuf-du-Pape was the summer retreat of the 14th-century Avignon popes. The remains of their château overlook the Rhône Valley. Only one tower and a stretch of walls survive.

Most visitors are attracted by the area's highly refined wines (the popes are thought to have established the first vineyards here). There is a bemusing choice of *domaines* where you can taste this prized wine, which benefits from a favourable microclimate and a ground cover of large rounded pebbles that enables the grapes to reach a very high degree of maturity.

Nearby, on the opposite bank of the Rhône, is Roquemaure, another wine village with papal connnections, well-preserved old houses, a 13th-century church and a ruined castle.

Musée du Vin

The museum traces the history of wine in the area, with displays of medieval equipment (includes a free wine tasting). *Caves Laurent Charles Brotte. Tel: 04 90 83 70 07; www.brotte.com. Open: winter, 9am–noon & 2–6pm; summer, 9am–1pm & 2–7pm. Free admission.*

Châteauneuf-du-Pape is on the D17 between Avignon and Orange.

Dentelles de Montmirail

This striking line of hills flanks the eastern side of the Rhône Valley for 15km (9 miles) between Vaison-la-Romaine and Beaumes-de-Venise. Rising to 734m (2,446ft),

they should be dwarfed by the 1,909-m (6,263-ft) summit of Mont Ventoux. Yet their strange, fiercely jagged profile – a complete contrast to Ventoux's smooth, uniform mass – imparts a presence almost matching that of their lofty neighbour.

The range takes its name from *dentelle*, meaning lace: the needle-sharp peaks and spikes of limestone rock, forced upright by the movement of the earth's crust and eroded by the wind, were thought to resemble the pins on a lacemaking board. Their white-grey summits, rising above slopes and hidden valleys covered in a thick coat of pine, oak and scrub, attract walkers, climbers, naturalists and painters – and, in autumn, seekers of wild mushrooms. While it is best to explore the Dentelles on foot, the D90 linking Beaumes-de-Venise with Malaucène is a spectacularly scenic road that loops through the mountains. The western slopes are dotted with famous Côtes-du-Rhône wine villages – Gigondas, Vacqueyras, Sablet and Séguret.

The jagged Dentelles de Montmirail are a challenge to rock climbers

Fontaine de Vaucluse

Few visitors see Fontaine de Vaucluse at its most spectacular. The best time to visit this dramatic natural phenomenon is in the winter or spring, when the source of the River Sorgue, fed by rainwater from the Vaucluse Plateau above, rises from a deep hole at the base of a sheer cliff and tumbles over giant boulders down a narrow ravine.

But even in summer, when the source has retreated to a still, ominous pool beneath the cliff face leaving the river bed above bone dry, it is still an awesome sight. The Vaucluse Fountain is one of the most powerful resurgent springs in the world (it can pump water over its lip at the rate of 150,000 litres/ 33,000 gallons per second) and has been traced underground to a depth of over 300m (984ft) by a remote-controlled submarine.

Fontaine de Vaucluse's magnetic personality has attracted the inevitable clutch of gift shops and souvenir stalls, which line the riverside walk from the car parks to the resurgence. Summer crowds can be a problem, so plan your visit for early in the day – or lunchtime, if you can stand the heat. On your way to the resurgence call in at the paper mill, where high-quality paper is still made the traditional way with the help of a giant water wheel.

Ecomusée du Gouffre

This riverside visitor centre, in which an underground cave system has been re-created, explains the local spelaeology and the discoveries made at the fountain. *Maison du Tourisme, tel: 04 90 20 32 22. Open: Feb–mid-Nov 9.30am–12.30pm &*
2–6pm. Conducted tours in French. Admission charge.

Musée Pétrarque

Documents and books relating to the life of the 14th-century poet Petrarch can be seen in this small museum, together with a collection of modern art. *Rive gauche de la Sorgue. Tel: 04 90 20 37 20. Open: Apr–May, Wed–Mon, 10am–noon & 2–6pm; June–Sept, Wed–Mon, 10am–12.30pm & 1.30–6pm; 1–15 Oct, Wed–Mon, 10am–noon & 2–6pm; 15 Oct–15, Wed–Mon, Nov 10am–noon & 2–5pm. Closed: mid-Nov–Apr. Admission charge.*

Fontaine de Vaucluse is on the D25, 24km (15 miles) southeast of Carpentras.

Gordes

Gordes is almost too good to be true. Overlooking the blue hills of the Luberon, this village of honey-coloured stone houses clings to a south-facing cliff on the edge of the Vaucluse Plateau. Renovated rustic dwellings, villas and discreet hotels, each one complete with the obligatory swimming pool, help create an idyllic vision of Provençal life. The village is much favoured by the French élite – actors, politicians, media personalities and artists. This status is confirmed by the breathtaking prices displayed by local *immobiliers* (estate agents).

Despite its chic nature, Gordes's historic fabric shines through. From the medieval château in the centre of the village, steep cobbled alleyways, lined with an incongruous mixture of fashionable boutiques, immaculate holiday homes and yet-to-be-restored houses, weave a confusing path down the precipitous hillside.

Abbaye de Sénanque

The medieval abbey, one of three founded by the Cistercians in Provence, is still in use and also open to the public for guided tours in French.
About 4km (2 1/2 miles) north of Gordes on the D177. Tel: 04 90 72 05 72; www. senanque.fr. Telephone for opening hours. Closed: Sun morning.
Admission charge.

Château de Gordes

This solid-looking castle, flanked by round corner towers, dates from 1031 and was rebuilt in 1525. The castle's Renaissance interior houses the Musée Pol Mara, which displays the work of Belgian artist Pol Mara (1920–98).
Village centre. Tel: 04 90 72 02 75. Open: daily, 10am–noon, 2–6pm.
Admission charge.

Village des Bories

Although the *bories* (dry-stone huts) in this amazing village and museum of rural life are prehistoric in appearance, they were in fact built between 200 and 500 years ago. The curving, cone-like roofs display craftsmanship of the highest order.
Signposted about 3km (2 miles) southwest of Gordes off the D2. Tel: 04 90 72 03 48. Open: daily, 9am–sunset.
Admission charge.

Gordes is off the D2, 20km (12 miles) west of Apt.

L'Isle-sur-la-Sorgue

Antique hunters and lovers of bric-a-brac spend hours pouring through the myriad furniture and decorative bargains in this delightful canal-side town, once noted for its fishing and fabrics industry. Some of its old water wheels can still be seen. The weekend market, renowned throughout the country, adds a further dimension to its genteel air.
About 18km (11 miles) south of Carpentras.

Fontaine de Vaucluse, where the River Sorgue emerges from its underground source

Orange

Visitors arrive with preconceptions of a Roman town *par excellence* and are never disappointed with Orange's awesome Théâtre Antique (amphitheatre) and the wonderfully decorative Arc de Triomphe Roman archway. But take these ancient monuments away, and you are left with a fairly ordinary Provençal town blessed with a traffic system that defies any form of logic.

The 1st-century BC Roman triumphal arch in Orange

The medieval heart of Orange, just north of the Théâtre Antique, though it lacks the personality of other old town centres in this part of the world, is a pleasant place, with open, fountained squares, cafés and shops. To the south, on a high bluff above the Théâtre Antique, is the Parc de la Colline St-Eutrope, with a beautiful viewpoint overlooking the town, the rich vineyards of the Rhône Plain, and the Marcoule nuclear power station. This outcrop was the site of a castle (now in ruins) of the princes of Orange-Nassau, destroyed in 1663.

Despite the name, it was in another, much earlier era that Orange's true identity was established. The Romans founded a colony here in 35 BC, leaving the town with a unique legacy. The amphitheatre that goes back to that era is today said to be the best-preserved Roman theatre in the world. We have Maurice, son of William the Silent, to thank for its survival. He incorporated the theatre's massive wall into the town's fortification, to the benefit of both. Orange's Arc de Triomphe is another remarkable survivor.

Arc de Triomphe

Built in about 20 BC, this triple-arched monument stands 22m (72ft) high and is decorated with scenes recalling the Roman conquest of Gaul.
On the northern approach to the town – follow avenue de l'Arc de Triomphe from the centre.

Cathédrale Notre-Dame-de-Nazareth

This Romanesque cathedral, originally founded in 529, suffered great damage during the 16th-century Wars of Religion. Look out for the ancient carvings on the south porch.
Along rue Notre-Dame off rue Victor-Hugo.

Musée Municipale

Exhibits from Orange's Roman and medieval past include a fascinating Roman land survey and artefacts from the ruined castle. Local traditions and painting are also represented.
Rue Madeleine-Roch. Tel: 04 90 51 17 60. Open: Jan, Feb, Nov & Dec, daily, 9am–5pm; Mar & Oct, daily, 9am–6pm; Apr–Sept, daily, 9am–7pm. Admission charge.

Théâtre Antique
(Roman Amphitheatre)

This theatre, built during the reign of Augustus, is an awesome sight. Looking down from the steep-sided semicircle of terraced seats to the stage, you gaze at virtually the same backdrop that must have caught the imagination of audiences 2,000 years ago. The stage wall still stands 36m (118ft) high, decorated with columns, niches, frescoes and a large, suitably imperious statue of Augustus. The theatre's superb acoustics continue to be put to good use. Audiences of 10,000 gather here during Orange's famous summer festival of opera and choral music, though today's patrons are not seated according to rank.

Beside the amphitheatre are the ruins of a huge gymnasium, baths and temple complex, with three, 180-m (591-ft) running tracks and a raised platform for gladiatorial combat.

Place des Frères-Mounet. Open: as for Musée Municipale. Admission charge.

The House of Orange

In 1572 William the Silent, Prince of Orange and Nassau, laid the foundation for the House of Orange when he was elected William I, Stadholder of the Low Countries – the Netherlands. The title passed on to his sons, who allied the House of Orange through marriage to the other powerful Protestant families of Europe: the Hohenzollerns in Prussia and the Stuarts in England.

Orange's great Roman theatre is still in use, notably for the town's summer music festival

The rock of the surrounding country gives Roussillon's buildings their red-gold shades

Roussillon

Roussillon's architecture is a mirror image of its surroundings. The deep reds, yellows, rusty oranges and other burnished tones of its houses reflect the different shades of ochre rock found in its surrounding hills. This area's soft rocks have been quarried and mined since prehistoric times for their natural dye. Mining peaked in the late 1920s, when 40,000 tons of ochre were exported from the region. By the early 1950s the industry was in terminal decline, and the last ochre was mined in Roussillon in 1958.

The village's vibrantly coloured dwellings, arranged haphazardly in narrow, winding streets around a pronounced hill, have given it a new lease of life: Roussillon is now a place that everyone wants to see, paint and photograph. Park your car at the approach and follow rue de l'Arcade to a superb viewpoint overlooking the Vaucluse Plateau, Mont Ventoux, the Coulon Valley and the Luberon Mountains. From vantage points south and southeast of the village, you can gaze over the **Aiguilles du Val des Fées** (Needles of Fairies' Valley) and the **Chaussée des Géants** (Giant's Causeway), strangely weathered areas of rust-red rocks and cliffs.
Roussillon is off the N100, about 10km (6 miles) northwest of Apt.

Rustrel Colorado

The explosive intensity of colours in the abandoned, canyon-like ochre quarries of Rustrel Colorado has to be seen to be believed. Ranging from blood-red to bright yellow, exposed cliff faces and weathered pinnacles consisting entirely of crumbly, sandy rock fill the valley south of the village of Rustrel. A number of trails lead into this other-worldly place. The easiest access is from the car parks beside the River Doua southwest and southeast of Rustrel, starting points for well-defined paths into the Colorado.
Rustrel Colorado is off the D22, about 8km (5 miles) northeast of Apt.

Sault

Standing at an exhilarating 765m (2,510ft), Sault displays yet another of Provence's many faces. On the high, open Vaucluse Plateau with sweeping vistas westwards to Mont Ventoux, Sault and its surroundings have an almost Alpine air. The fields beneath this unpretentious, easy-going village are a patchwork of purple in high summer, when the lavender is in full bloom. The entire village is swamped in its sweet fragrance during the annual Lavender

Festival, held in mid-August. Lavender cultivation and distillation is an important part of the local economy. So too is the manufacture of nougat. The Boyer family of Sault claim that their nougat, not the better-known Montélimar variety, is the real thing. *Sault is on the eastern approach to Mont Ventoux, 41km (25 miles) east of Carpentras.*

Séguret

Séguret is one of those impossibly picturesque villages that only the French seem capable of creating. Mellow, wheat-coloured houses with terracotta tiled roofs cling to a steep slope above the vineyards of the northern Vaucluse. So well is Séguret integrated into its

Golden-stoned square and fountain in the unspoilt medieval village of Séguret

surroundings that when the sun strikes directly on to its stonework it almost disappears, chameleon-like, into the rocky background of the Dentelles de Montmirail (*see p35*).

The village's ridiculously narrow streets were not made for cars. From the car park at the western approach, walk up into the village through the ancient gateway to the 15th-century Mascarons Fountain. Over the last couple of decades, Séguret has been 'discovered' by artists and visitors, yet it has managed to avoid the commercial excesses of other hill villages. A medieval atmosphere still pervades its cobbled alleyways, vaulted passageways, nooks and crannies. Each Christmas the 12th-century church is decorated with *santons*, intricately detailed figurines depicting the Nativity (*see p125*). *Santons* and Séguret go together: there are a number of makers in the village, one of whom has an enchanting display from around the world. *Séguret is off the D977, 10km (6 miles) southwest of Vaison-la-Romaine.*

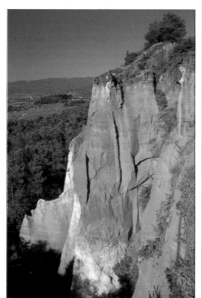

Roussillon's ochre-rich cliffs provide a unique coloured stone for its buildings

Lavender and flowers

The flowers of Provence are amongst its greatest treasures. Their heady mix of colours and scents makes a vivid impression on the senses, not only catching the eye of the casual observer but providing inspiration for the artist and a fertile field of study for the naturalist.

Nature is at its most prodigal in April and May, when sheets of spring flowers cloak the fields and hills. High summer brings out the gaudy brilliance of the sunflower, which Van Gogh captured so well on canvas. But it is typical of the sheer unexpectedness of Provence that the region should also harbour the delicate beauty of the arctic flora that clings to the upper slopes of Mont Ventoux, despite the Mediterranean influences at the foot of the mountain.

The scent of lavender

It is, perhaps, the lavender that imprints itself most vividly upon the memory of the visitor. In this sun-soaked region it grows abundantly, staining the fields a delicate purple and scenting the air in July and August. This pungent scent is captured second-hand in the perfumes of Provence. Golden mimosa, jonquils, roses, thyme, violets and yellow broom are also gathered – some would say plundered – to provide the raw material for the perfumer's art. The flower markets also do a brisk trade in the towns and villages of Provence, and mimosa is cultivated for export in winter.

Hidden away

The *maquis* – not a single plant, but a community of dense Mediterranean brush – half-conceals an amazing variety of floral life, including

rosemary and juniper, tree heathers and broom. Orchids are plentiful in some districts. The herbs of Provence have not only played a central role in regional cuisine, but have traditionally provided remedies for many an ill.

No self-respecting resort is without that symbol of the Côte d'Azur, the palm tree. Other subtropical and exotic species, in gardens all along the Riviera, also take root in this sunny, sheltered habitat.

During World War II, when the French Resistance wanted a name that would symbolise their indomitable toughness, they turned to the hardy scrub plants of Provence, and called themselves the Maquis.

Provence in bloom is a sensory delight with acres of heady lavender as well as other flowers

Vaison-la-Romaine

Try to visit Vaison on a Tuesday morning, when the town holds one of the biggest street markets in Provence. Place de Montfort – Vaison's attractive central square – and almost all of the streets leading to it are filled with vendors of fruit, melons and olives, fishmongers, cheesemakers, antique dealers, painters, craftspeople, florists, musicians, entertainers and sellers of humble household items. This colourful, animated gathering is not a show put on for the tourists: markets are a way of life in Provence, and Vaison holds one of the best.

For the rest of the week, Vaison returns to its primary role as a calm and surprisingly cosmopolitan small Provençal town. It is popular with visitors on at least two counts: the town's location, in seductive, rolling countryside between the Rhône Valley and Mont Ventoux, and its underrated, magnificent Roman remains.

The Romans made a comfortable home for themselves in Vaison. You can still wander round the streets of their excavated town, or watch a summer

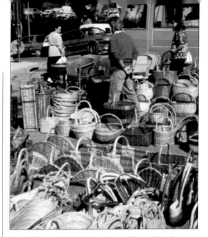

Everything sold at Vaison's weekly market is typical of Provence

concert in the 7,000-seat amphitheatre. The Romans' single-arched bridge survived the devastating floods in Vaison in the autumn of 1992, when unrelenting storms, held in place by Mont Ventoux, transformed the River Ouvèze into a tidal wave, swamping the lower town. Vaison's Haute-Ville (Upper Town) was untouched by the floodwater.

The rock above the Ouvèze is crowned by an abandoned castle, a wonderful viewpoint accessible by climbing through the narrow, cobbled streets of Old Vaison, a charming and

The medieval town of Vaison-la-Romaine climbs above the remains of a Roman city now fashionable place with fountains and fine Renaissance houses.

Ancienne Cathédrale Notre-Dame-de-Nazareth

Built on the foundations of a large Roman monument, this fine cathedral in Provençal Romanesque style dates from the 12th and 13th centuries. Its beautiful cloisters, attached to its northern wall, are particularly noteworthy.
Avenue Louis-Blanc. Open: as for the Ruines. Admission charge to cloisters.

Ruines Romaines

Such is the extent of these sprawling ruins that they are split into two sections – Quartier de Puymin and Quartier de la Villasse – divided by the avenue Général de Gaulle, which leads into the town centre. All in all, they give us a rare insight into ordinary, everyday life in the 1st century AD.

Quartier de Puymin, built around a small hill, contains the Théâtre Antique (amphitheatre), the Portique de Pompée (Pompey's Portico), a beautiful colonnaded area that probably served as a public garden, and the remains of residences both modest and grand. The museum, full of finds excavated in Vaison, is also located here.

Quartier de la Villasse contains an amazing paved main street, complete with drains and the remains of shops, together with baths, more gardens, large houses and colonnades.
Accessible off avenue de Général de Gaulle. Tel: 04 90 36 50 00 (mairie). Open: Mar–May, daily, 10am–12.30pm & 2–6pm; June–Sept, daily, 9.30am–6.30pm; Oct–Feb, daily,

Vaison-la-Romaine shelters the most complete Roman town to be discovered in France

10am–noon & 2–5pm. Guided visits in English from Easter to end Oct by appointment (tel: 04 90 36 50 48). Admission charge.
Vaison-la-Romaine is 29km (18 miles) north of Carpentras.

Vénasque

Vénasque sits astride a steep rock overlooking the Gorges de la Nesque. Its natural defensive position was augmented in medieval times by towers and walls, giving the pretty village an even more self-contained air. Its famous baptistery, probably dating from the 6th century, is one of France's oldest religious buildings. The 13th-century **Église de Notre-Dame** beside the baptistery is also of interest.

From Vénasque, you can follow a twisting road that climbs over the Vaucluse Plateau to another fascinating religious site, the Abbaye de Sénanque (*see p37*). Another place worth visiting nearby is **Pernes-les-Fontaines**, a working market town that preserves a wonderful array of old monuments, including medieval walls, a tower, gateways, chapels, Renaissance streets and, of course, fountains – 36 in all!
Vénasque is 11km (7 miles) southeast of Carpentras on the D4.

Tour: Mont Ventoux

Wherever you travel in the Vaucluse, you take Mont Ventoux with you. This towering landmark, 1,909m (6,263ft) high, is visible from all corners, its gleaming white summit of bare rock shimmering against the blue heat haze or suddenly – and ominously – cast into shadow by gathering storm clouds. Mont Ventoux, literally the Windy Mountain, is the intimidating presence in an otherwise seductive Provençal landscape. You would not want to be on Ventoux's summit when the *mistral* is blowing at a brutal 250kph (155mph). On the other hand, in sunny, calm weather, the views from the top are truly breathtaking. *Allow at least half a day for the tour.*

From Vaison-la-Romaine (see pp44–5) take the D938 to Malaucène.

1 Malaucène

Malaucène's pleasant main street is lined with plane trees, cafés and restaurants. The old town, a maze of alleyways, tall houses and fountains, preserves an authentic Provençal atmosphere. Malaucène's proximity to Mont Ventoux

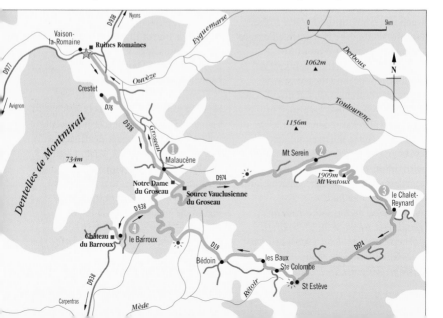

makes it a lively tourist centre in summer and a major base for hiking, riding and cycling expeditions. A short distance from the town, on the road up to Mont Ventoux, is La Groseau, a spring that emerges from a rocky fissure to form a clear pool surrounded by trees and picnic tables.

The D974 climbs through beautiful wooded countryside on the north-facing slopes of Ventoux. Up until the ski station of Mont Serein, the road is wide, with sweeping, well-engineered bends.

2 Mont Serein

At 1,445m (4,741ft), Mont Serein is a modest ski resort, busy at weekends in winter with skiers from Avignon (the mountain is usually snowcapped above 1,400m from December to March).

The final climb to the summit of Mont Ventoux from Mont Serein is the most spectacular part of the ascent. The road becomes narrower, the bends more severe – and the drops more vertiginous! For the final 300m (984ft) or so, the forests of pine, oak, cedar, beech and larch give way to a bare expanse of broken rock, a strange, barren environment. Stranger still are the monumental buildings and sinister-looking installations on the summit; these are used for telecommunications, air force radar and meteorological purposes. The panorama from the top is one of the best in Europe. On a clear day, looking down into the valley of the Toulourenc or across to the jagged peaks of the Alps gives a fleeting impression of flight.

From the summit, the D974 descends to Le Chalet-Reynard, Ventoux's smaller, southern ski station.

3 Le Chalet-Reynard

Before Le Chalet-Reynard, you will see a small roadside monument, usually garlanded by cycle tyres and inner tubes. This shrine is a homage to British cyclist Tommy Simpson, who suffered heart failure here on 13 July 1967 while competing in the Tour de France. It was one of the hottest days ever recorded in the race.

Continue on the D974 to Bédoin (see p32) and the scenic D19, which brings you to the D938. Here, you can take a short detour south to Le Barroux.

4 Le Barroux

The restored Château du Barroux (*tel: 04 90 62 35 21*), dating from the 12th century and remodelled in the 16th, stands on a rocky outcrop overlooking the village.

On the way back to Vaison, take another short detour along the D76 for Crestet, a picturesque village perched high above the valley of the Ouvèze. Hidden in the slopes beyond the village is a fascinating collection of woodland sculptures.

The summit of Mont Ventoux is used for telecommunications, radar and meteorology

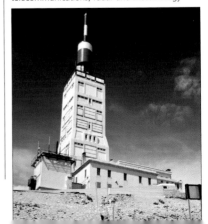

Bouches-du-Rhône

Bordered by the Durance to the north and the Rhône to the west, the Bouches-du-Rhône is one of the oldest inhabited regions of Provence, with some of the best monuments from Roman and medieval times. The mighty Rhône meets the Mediterranean amongst the reedy flatlands of the Camargue, a truly distinctive part of Provence with an identity all of its own. Elsewhere in this varied *département* there are low hills, fertile landscapes, busy commercial waterfronts and the first intimations of the glamorous Riviera coast.

The imposing ruins of Abbaye-de-Montmajour

Abbaye-de-Montmajour

This imposing ruin, which occupies a slight rise in the Rhône delta's flatlands northeast of Arles, is easily spotted. Looking more military than religious, it was founded in the 10th century by the Benedictines, an industrious group of monks who set about draining and reclaiming the marshlands of this low-lying area. In 1791, after a troubled few centuries, the abbey was sold and its assets stripped. Luckily, the people of Arles adopted the building in the 19th century, restoring it little by little.

Much remains from the abbey's early period: a 12th-century church with a fine vaulted crypt, cloisters (again 12th-century, but rebuilt in later times), monastic buildings, a tall, castellated abbey tower constructed to defend the abbey in 1369 and, next door to the tower, a tiny chapel carved out of the hillside.

On the D17 between Arles and Fontvieille. Tel: 04 90 54 64 17.
Open: May–Aug, daily, 10am–6pm; Sept–Apr, daily, 10am–5pm. Closed: Mon. Admission charge.

Abbaye de Silvacane

This 12th-century abbey is one of the Cistercians' 'three Provençal sisters' – the others being Sénanque (*see p37*) and Thoronet (*see p134*). From its setting above the River Durance, just a few kilometres from the village of La Roque-d'Anthéron, it looks across to the foothills of the Luberon.

The abbey's plain, uncluttered lines reflect the Cistercians' firm belief in simplicity. Its church, built into a steep slope, is devoid of any decoration. The daily routine of the monks is brought to life in some of the abbey's other buildings, which include a library, chapterhouse, warming house, dormitory and large refectory complete with pulpit. Following a period of decline, it became the village church for **La Roque-d'Anthéron** in the early 16th century, but was later abandoned.

On the D561, northeast of Salon-de-Provence. Tel: 04 42 50 41 69.
Open: June–Sept, daily, 10am–6pm; Oct–May, Wed–Sun, 10am–1pm & 2–5pm. Admission charge.

The fountain centrepiece
of La Rotonde

Aix-en-Provence

Take a stroll along cours Mirabeau on a warm summer's day and you could be forgiven for thinking that you are in Paris. The wide street, lined with pavement cafés, plane trees, mossy fountains and handsome 17th- and 18th-century buildings, must surely have been built for promenading. It captures the spirit of a city that is both youthful and dignified, stimulating and calming, stylish and historic. It is cosmopolitan, yet utterly French.

Aix, more than any other city in Provence, has an air of completeness. This may have something to do with its splendid situation poised between country and coast, with none of the rusticity of the former or the crass commercialism of the latter. It may also be due to a well-balanced blend of age groups – the youth of Aix's large student influx balanced against an affluent, worldly resident population. Whatever the reasons, it is a winning formula.

The city authorities have further enhanced Aix's intrinsic appeal by treating the historic centre with loving care and attention. Wherever you look, you will be reminded of Aix's historic status as capital of Provence, a position it held from the 12th century to the French Revolution.

Start your exploration at La Rotonde, a monumental roundabout with a fabulous fountained centrepiece. From here, walk along cours Mirabeau, which more or less acts as the southern boundary to Aix's historic heart (though the Mazarin Quarter, built between 1645 and 1651 by Archbishop Michel Mazarin, lies further south again).

Take any of the streets north and you are soon in the Aix of old. Place d'Albertas, for example, has a lovely cobbled courtyard and fountain flanked by 18th-century houses with wrought-iron balconies. Place Richelme, the site of a daily vegetable market, is another pleasant open space, next door to the even more spacious place de l'Hôtel de Ville. There are, perhaps, too many immaculate open spaces to appreciate them all in one visit. Architecture buffs will be similarly satiated with an overload of richly decorated 16th- to 18th-century mansions – the Hôtel de Ville, for instance, its classical features carved into warm stone.

Atelier Cézanne (Cézanne's Studio)
Impressionist painter Paul Cézanne (1839–1906) was inspired by the light, colour and surroundings of his birthplace, Aix. His studio has been left as it was at his death.
9 avenue Paul-Cézanne. Tel: 04 42 21 06 53; www.atelier-cezanne.com.

*Open: Apr–May, daily, 10am–noon &
2–6pm; June–Sept, daily, 10am–7pm;
Oct–Mar, daily, 10am–noon & 2–5pm.
Admission charge.*

Cathédrale St-Sauveur
Spanning the 5th to 16th centuries, this
fascinating religious site – a mixture of
ornate and restrained influences – is a
lesson in ecclesiastical architecture.
Filled with medieval art treasures, it also
boasts delightful Romanesque cloisters
displaying spiralling, flowing stonecarving of the highest order.
*At the north end of rue Gaston-de-
Saporta.*

Fondation Vasarely
The exciting work of 20th-
century artist Victor Vasarely is
difficult to categorise.
A visit to his arts and architecture
centre is a stimulating experience.
*Avenue Marcel-Pagnol, Jas-de-
Bouffan. Tel: 04 42 20 01 09.
www.fondationvasarely.com.
Open: Mon–Sat, 10am–6pm.
Admission charge.*

Musée d'Histoire Naturelle
(Museum of Natural History)
Important collections include
rare dinosaur eggs.
*6 rue Espariat. Tel: 04 42 27 91 27.
Open: Wed–Sat, 10am–noon &
1–5pm. Admission charge.*

Musée des Tapisseries
(Tapestry Museum)
Famous tapestries and panels
displayed in a former
archbishops' palace.

*28 place des Martyrs-de-la-Résistance.
Tel: 04 42 23 09 91. Open: Wed–Mon,
10am–noon & 2–6pm (1.30–7pm in
winter). Admission charge.*

Musée du Vieil Aix
(Museum of Old Aix)
The museum recalls Aix's aristocratic
past and popular traditions.
*17 rue Gaston-de-Saporta. Tel: 04 42 21
43 55. Open: Tue–Sun, 10am–noon &
2.30–5pm (till 6pm in summer).
Admission charge.*

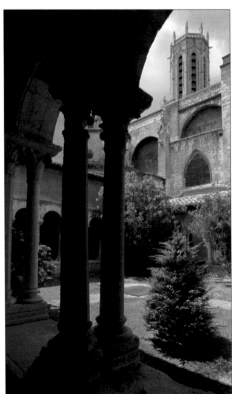

Shaded cloisters at the ancient Cathédrale St-Sauveur

Arles

Visitors attracted to Arles on the strength of the town's Roman past and the canvases of Vincent Van Gogh, its most celebrated resident, might expect to find a surfeit of upmarket shops and expensive cafés. But the town wears its fame lightly. Despite streets packed with monuments and museums, Arles maintains an honest, everyday quality.

Roman theatre: from fortress to township

The Romans established a major base here and the town continued to prosper in medieval times as an important trading and religious centre, and base for the Counts of Provence. Vincent Van Gogh arrived in Arles in 1888 and sang its praises to his colleague Paul Gauguin.

The Alyscamps
Wooded avenues of ancient tombs and mausoleums line this early Christian necropolis southeast of the town centre.
Ave des Alyscamps. Tel: 04 90 49 38 20. Open: Nov–Feb, daily, 10–11.30am & 2–4.30pm; Mar–Apr, daily, 9–11.30am & 2–5.30pm; May–Sept, daily, 9am–6pm; Oct, daily, 9–11.30am & 2–5.30pm. Admission charge.

Arènes (Roman Amphitheatre)
This enormous oval, dating from the end of the 1st century, became a fortress in medieval times. It was later transformed into a small township of 200 houses. Nineteenth-century restoration has largely returned it to its former glory, though its third floor has disappeared.
Rond-Point des Arènes. Tel: 04 90 49 38 20. Open: May–Sept, daily, 9am–6pm; Mar, Apr & Oct, daily, 9am–5.30pm; Nov–Feb, daily, 10am–4.30pm. Admission charge.

Fondation Vincent Van Gogh
Works by leading contemporary artists, sculptors and photographers pay homage here to the great painter.
Palais de Luppé, 26 Rond-Point des Arènes. Tel: 04 90 49 94 04; www.fondationvangogh-arles.com. Open: Apr–June, daily, 10am–6pm; July–Sept, daily, 10am–7pm; Oct–Mar, Tue–Sun, daily, 11am–5pm. Admission charge.

Musée d' Arles Antique
In a striking, contemporary building, ancient Arles comes to life through a superb collection of sarcophagi, sculpture and architectural details. Incorporating exhibits from the former Museum of Christian Art, this is a spacious and well-displayed museum.
Presqu'ille du Cirque Romain. Tel: 04 90 18 88 88. Open: Apr–Oct, daily, 9am–7pm; Nov–Mar, daily, 10am–5pm. Admission charge.

Musée Réattu
Founded by the painter Réattu (1760–1833), the museum is famous for its Picassos.
Rue du Grande Prieuré. Tel: 04 90 49 37 58. Open: Nov–Feb, daily, 1–5pm;

Mar–Apr & Oct, daily, 10am–noon & 2–5pm; May–Sept, daily, 10am–noon & 2–6.30pm. Admission charge.

Museon Arlaten

Poet Frédéric Mistral established this museum reflecting traditional Provençal life, crafts and customs at the turn of the 20th century.
Rue de la République. Tel: 04 90 93 58 11. Open: June–Aug, daily, 9.30am–noon & 2–5.30pm; Apr, May & Sept, Wed–Sun, 9.30am–noon & 2–5pm. Admission charge.

Primatiale St-Trophime

The cathedral's main doorway is probably the most accomplished example of 12th-century Provençal stonecarving in existence. The elaborate decorations are, literally, of biblical proportions.
Place de la République. Tel: 04 90 49 38 20. Cathedral open: daily, 10am–noon & 2–6pm. Free admission.
Cloisters open: May–Sept, daily, 9am–6pm; Mar, Apr & Oct, daily, 9am–5.30pm; Nov–Feb, daily, 10am–4.30pm. Admission charge.

Théâtre Antique (Roman Theatre)

There is not much antiquity left at this open-air theatre, but it is a pleasant venue for summer performances.
Rue de la Calade (close to the Arènes). Tel: 04 90 49 36 74. Open: Nov–Feb, daily, 10am–11.30am & 2–4.30 pm; Mar–Apr & Oct, daily, 9–11.30am & 2–5.30pm; June–Sept, daily, 9am–6pm. Admission charge.

Thermes de Constantin (Baths of Constantine)

Dating from the 4th century, these baths are all that remain of a Roman palace.

Rue Dominique-Maïsto. Tel: 04 90 49 36 74. Open: Nov–Feb, daily, 10am–11.30am & 2–4.30pm; Mar–Apr & Oct, daily, 9–11.30am & 2–5.30pm; June–Sept, daily, 9am–6pm. Admission charge.

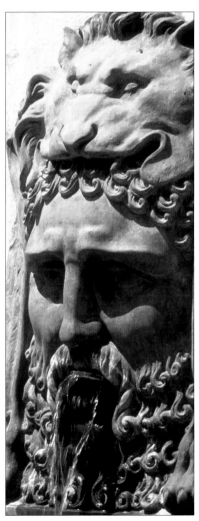

A detail of the fountain, place de la République

Walk: Arles

Arles looks after its walkers well. The places of interest, mostly within a relatively small area, are bounded by the mighty Rhône to the north, the Arènes (Roman amphitheatre) to the east, and the Espace Van Gogh to the west. To make it even easier, all main sites are well signposted.

Allow half a day for the walk: extra time for museum visits.

Begin the walk at the Office de Tourisme on boulevard des Lices. Walk along rue Jean-Jaurès to place de la République.

1 Place de la République

Place de la République, Arles' central square, is a large, open space where historic architecture, for once, is without the usual forest of street-café parasols. The uncluttered square's impressive dimensions, and the stature of the buildings that surround it, are immediately apparent. Overlooking the fountain and Roman obelisk are the Clock Tower and Hôtel de Ville (Town Hall), its classical 17th-century façade reminiscent of Versailles. To one side is the Ancienne Église Ste-Anne. But the square's chief glory is the wonderfully decorative main doorway of the Primatiale St-Trophîme.

Rue de la Calade leads to the Théâtre Antique (Roman theatre), Arènes (Roman amphitheatre) and Fondation Vincent Van Gogh.

2 Arènes

The Arènes may not seem quite as high as you anticipated: its third storey has disappeared and, adding to its denuded

appearance, the pavement around the monument is elevated for much of the way. Halfway around the Arènes, at the place la Major, visit the **Collégiale Notre-Dame-la-Major**, a Romanesque collegiate church built close to surviving sections of the city ramparts.

Opposite the main steps to the Arènes, follow rue du l'Amphithéâtre (or the prettier, adjacent rue Voltaire, in which case take two left turns to get back to rue du 4 Septembre), turning left into rue du 4 Septembre. Turn right by the Église St-Julien along rue St-Julien to the riverbank of the Rhône (note the remains of the Roman bridge to the north). A ramped pathway runs along the riverside to the Musée Réattu – the entrance is along rue du Grande Prieuré.

3 Thermes de Constantin

Only a short distance from the Musée Réattu are the Thermes de Constantin (Baths of Constantine), accessible along rue Dominique-Maïsto.

Continue along this street for rue de l'Hôtel-de-Ville, turning right into rue des Arènes, which brings you to place du Forum.

4 Place du Forum

This small, charming square, lined with cafés and restaurants, is Arles' social hub. On a clear summer's night, it is easy to see where Van Gogh's inspiration for *Café Evening* came from. A statue of Provençal poet and Nobel Prize-winner Frédéric Mistral stands amongst plane trees, close to the Hôtel Nord-Pinus, whose façade partly consists of two columns from a 2nd-century Roman temple.

Leave place du Forum by rue du Palais, turning right along rue Balze. Then turn left into rue Frédéric-Mistral, then left again into rue de la République – one of Arles' main shopping streets – for the Museon Arlaten. Close to the museum, along rue du Président-Wilson, is the Espace Van Gogh.

5 Espace Van Gogh

Espace Van Gogh, inaugurated in 1989, is the old Hôtel-Dieu hospital in which the artist spent time after cutting off his ear lobe. It has now been converted into a cultural centre with garden and a courtyard with small workshops and souvenir shops, all painted in suitably vibrant colours (*open: Tue, Wed, Fri & Sat*).

Arles

Van Gogh

The name of the Dutch painter Vincent Van Gogh (1853–90) is ineradicably linked with Provence. The region shimmers with heightened colour and vibrancy in the loud, swirling canvases he painted here towards the end of his troubled life.

Van Gogh, the son of a pastor, trained for the ministry himself, but he was re-proached for 'excessive zeal' by his superiors when he gave many of his possessions to the poor. He decided to become an artist and was kept alive principally by a regular allowance from his younger brother Théo.

bewitched by its dazzling light and colours, and rented a house in Arles in 1888. Inspired by the idea of an artists' colony, he persuaded his friend Paul Gauguin to join him, but the two soon fell out. After a fierce row, Van Gogh cut off the lobe of his right ear and sent it to a prostitute in an envelope.

Blossoming creativity

Despite – or perhaps because of – his emotional state, his 14 months in Arles were the most productive of his life. During this short period, he produced hundreds of paintings and drawings. Van

The lure of the south

Self-taught as an artist, he was influenced by the new French Impressionist movement led by Monet, Renoir and Degas and lived in the Montmartre area of Paris for two years. He then moved to the South of France,

Gogh was never popular in the town, where he was jeered at as a 'madman', and none of his works can be found in the local art museums. The sunflowers and cypresses he depicted so vividly still grow in abundance, however, and his personal experience of Provence is captured in such works as the portrait of

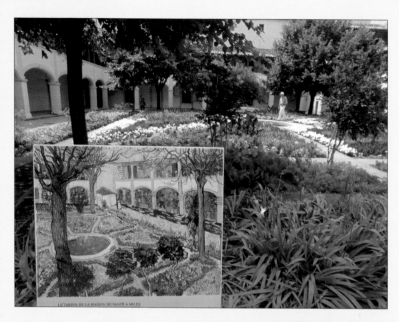

LE JARDIN DE LA MAISON DE SANTÉ A ARLES

his friend Roulin the postman, his painting of his bedroom in Arles, and the swirling colours of his magical *Starry Night* series.

In 1889, fear of madness prompted him to commit himself voluntarily to an asylum in St-Rémy-de-Provence, where he was allowed to paint in the gardens. Later he moved to Auvers-sur-Oise in northern France, but shot himself in the chest in July 1890.

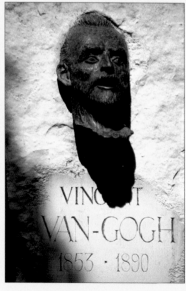

Facing page: the artist himself – from a poster in Arles
Above: Van Gogh's painting (inset) of the Hôtel-Dieu, where he spent his last days
Right: memorial to the artist in Arles

Les Baux-de-Provence

Hundreds of thousands of visitors pour through the entrance to Les Baux each year, making it one of Provence's most popular attractions, so it does get extremely busy. Nonetheless, to miss Les Baux is to miss a unique and stirring sight. In a country of countless fortified towns and villages, it ranks among the finest. Its size alone makes it special. Les Baux occupies a narrow spur of land almost 1km ($^1/_2$ mile) long, flanked by sheer-sided cliffs. But this offshoot of the Alpilles range of hills is not famous simply for its natural attributes.

The typical, narrow streets of Les Baux-de-Provence

This protected mini-plateau is the site of a remarkable medieval ghost town. At one time, this citadel was a town of 6,000 inhabitants. Throughout the medieval period, Les Baux and its bellicose independent rulers had a troublesome reputation.

In 1632, the French monarchy's patience finally broke and Les Baux's castle and ramparts were demolished. Its crestfallen population migrated to land reclaimed from the marshes. It then lay forgotten for centuries until the discovery of bauxite – the aluminium ore that takes its name from the town – in the locality in the 19th century.

Nowadays, Les Baux relies on tourism. The lower village, the 'living town', is the focus of all the commercial attention, though it still contains some fine old buildings. Place St-Vincent is a lovely, shady square, with views across to the **Val d'Enfer** (Valley of Hell, so called because of its weirdly eroded, jagged countenance). Ranged around the square are the 12th-century Église St-

Vincent, the 17th-century **Chapelle des Pénitents-Blancs** and the 16th-century **Hôtel des Porcelets**, which displays works of contemporary art. The **Hôtel de Manville**, a 16th-century building with beautiful Renaissance windows, now serves as the town hall.

Cathédrale d'Images

A short distance northwest of the village on the D27 is the Cathédrale d'Images. Here, the vast caverns of the old bauxite quarries serve as a unique three-dimensional screen for an inventive sound and light show which projects images on to every available surface. *Tel: 04 90 54 38 65; www.cathedrale-images.com. Open: Mar–Jan, daily, 10am–6pm; Apr–Sept, daily, 10am–7pm.*

Ville Morte

The undoubted highlight of a visit to Les Baux is the Deserted Village, or Ville Morte. This strange place, on the higher ground to the east and south, is a sprawl of stumpy, intriguing remains that seem to grow out of the bare, dazzlingly white limestone rock. The entire area is sealed off, accessible only through the Musée Lapidaire in the lower village (entry by payment). The museum displays artefacts excavated locally together with a presentation of the history of the citadel. On entering the Ville Morte, one of the first sites you come to is the Romanesque Chapelle St-Blaise. From here, walk to the southern tip of the plateau to the monument of the poet Charloun Rieu. Here you can take in an all-encompassing viewpoint south to Arles and the Camargue as far as Stes-Maries-de-la-Mer.

The main defensive sites are at the opposite end of the plateau, beyond the Tour Sarrasine (Saracen Tower). The shell of Les Baux's once mighty castle, demolished in the 17th century, still captures the imagination (there are more

magnificent panoramas from its 13th-century keep and the Tour Paravelle).
Château des Baux en Provence.
Tel: 04 90 54 55 56. Open: spring, daily,
9am–6.30pm; summer, daily, 9am–7.30pm;
autumn, daily, 9am–6pm; winter, daily,
9.30am–5pm. Admission charge.

The Penitents
The Middle Ages saw the formation of penitent brotherhoods, mostly charitable organisations patronised by noblemen and even royalty – partly, perhaps, to make a favourable impression through public penance and good deeds and thus massage their consciences; partly to help each other. Each fraternity had a different-coloured habit and hood, by which they were identified during processions. The White, Grey and Black Penitents all had chapels in Avignon. In the 16th century both Charles IX and Henri III walked barefoot through Avignon in the white hood that identified the White Penitents.

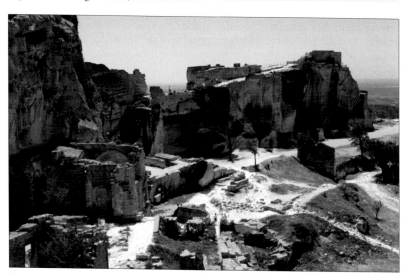

The atmospheric Ville Morte of Les Baux rewards the stiff climb from the town below

The Camargue

The Camargue is unique. This strange, flat, lagoon-like delta is an unfathomable mixture of land and water; it is difficult to discern where land begins and water ends. The Camargue's major feature is the Étang de Vaccarès, a large lagoon that is the focal point for the Parc Naturel Régional de Camargue. The entire area is bounded by two rivers, the Grand and the Petit Rhône, and riddled with irrigation channels, ditches and dikes.

Crane and flamingoes, very much at home in the watery landscape of the Camargue

Human settlement is thin on the ground, restricted mainly to the Camargue's hardy *gardians* (herdsmen). Humans apart, this indeterminate environment teems with wildlife. The Camargue is one giant nature reserve, home to stick-legged flamingoes and badgers, seabirds and marshbirds, frogs and pond turtles, water snakes and wild boars. To this list is added the famous white horses and the bulls, essential elements in the local Camarguais culture (*see p63*). It would be irresponsible not to mention another, less appealing member of the local fauna: the mosquito. In summer, anywhere away from a sea breeze, you will need the protection of a potent insect repellent. The Camargue's mosquitoes have been known to drive strong men crazy!

Aigues-Mortes

Fortified Aigues-Mortes has a remarkably well-preserved ring of walls. Their survival was due more to benign neglect than anything else, for the town was a forgotten backwater for centuries.

Tour de Constance (Constance Tower) and Ramparts

This 13th-century tower is a massive, 40-m (131-ft) high keep in the northwestern corner of Aigues-Mortes' rectangular fortifications. From the top there is a terrific view across the town and the Camargue.
Tel: 04 66 53 61 55. Open: Oct–Mar 10am–5.30pm; Apr–Sept 10am–7pm. Admission charge.
Aigues-Mortes is 42km (26 miles) southwest of Nîmes.

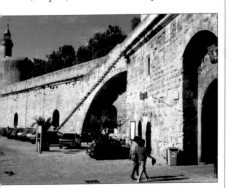
Aigues-Mortes, built as a port, is still largely contained within its 13th-century ramparts

Centre d'Information du Parc

Based alongside the **Étang de Ginès** (Ginès Lagoon), this excellent centre illustrates the Camargue's flora and fauna through exhibitions and real life: electric-pink flamingoes and other wildlife can be seen from the huge observation window. There are similar centres – La Capelière (*tel: 04 90 97 00 97*) and Domaine de la Palissade (*tel: 04 42 86 81 28*) – on the eastern side of Étang de Vaccarès.
Pont de Gau. Tel: 04 90 97 86 32; www.parc-camargue.fr. Open: Apr–Sept, Sat–Thur, 9.30am–5pm. Closed: Fri, Oct–Mar. Free admission.

Château d'Avignon

Take a guided tour of this opulently furnished château, which stands in beautiful grounds.
At Albaron. Tel: 04 90 97 58 58 for information. Open: summer, Wed–Mon, 10am–5pm. Closed: winter. Admission charge.

La Grande-Motte

Purpose-built La Grande-Motte is an ultra-modern seaside resort of bold triangular apartment blocks which, on first impression, look as if they would be more at home on a snowy French Alp. Closer acquaintance reveals imaginative landscaping that makes it less intimidating.
La Grande-Motte is 12km (7 miles) west of Aigues-Mortes.

Mas du Pont de Rousty

The **Musée Camarguais** is located at this old *mas* (farmhouse). It covers the history and human activity of the area, and has a 3.5-km (2¼-mile) countryside trail.

The hardy bulls of Camargue are a mainstay of the region's economy

On the D570 approximately 9km (5½ miles) southwest of Arles. Tel: 04 90 97 10 82. Open: Wed–Mon, 10.15am–4.45pm. Admission charge.

Parc Ornithologique du Pont de Gau

Alongside the Centre d'Information du Parc, this park has aviaries plus many well-signposted trails for bird spotters.
Tel: 04 90 97 82 62; www.parcornithologique.com. Open: Apr–Sept, daily, 9am–sunset; Oct–Mar, daily, 10am–sunset. Admission charge.

Saintes-Maries-de-la-Mer

This popular seaside resort is too commercialised for some tastes. Its white-painted, boxy dwellings are more reminiscent of Spain than France, an impression reinforced by the flamenco guitarist street musicians. The town is a famous gathering place for the gypsies on 24 and 25 May each year, when they celebrate their patron saint Sarah (*see pp14–15*).
Saintes-Maries-de-la-Mer is 33km (21 miles) southeast of Aigues-Mortes.

Tour: the Camargue

Unlike other parts of Provence, the scenery in the Camargue is not stunning. It is a flat, reedy, marshy and watery place. Here, the wildlife takes priority. You will not even have to look particularly hard, for the prolific birdlife, celebrated white horses and bulls, insouciant in their protected habitat, are all visible from the road. Make sure you leave yourself enough time to experience this area as it should be experienced – on foot or horseback. There are plenty of opportunities for both along the route. The previous pages give details on places to visit. One final word of advice: theft from cars is particularly rife in this area, so make sure you lock valuables out of sight.

The tour begins at Arles. Allow a full day.

Leave Arles on the D570. This will take you to the Mas du Pont de Rousty, which is a visitor centre for the Parc and will give you a good, all-round introduction to the Camargue. Continue along the D570 to Albaron, turning left along the D37. After 4km (2 1/2 miles), bear right on the C5 for Méjanes.

1 Méjanes

Méjanes is a popular spot with visitors. This large complex offers horse riding, bullfighting (*see box*) and rides on a narrow-gauge railway.

Return to the D570, turning left towards Stes-Maries-de-la-Mer. Shortly, you will come to the entrance to the Château d'Avignon. Continue on to Pont de Gau, stopping off at the Centre d'Information du Parc Naturel Régional de Camargue and the next-door Parc Ornithologique.

2 Pont de Gau

At Pont de Gau and along the road into Stes-Maries-de-la-Mer, there are many stables at which you can hire horses. Stes-Maries' best beaches, which stretch for many kilometres, are found to the east of the town, and there is a good choice of boat trips.

Leave Stes-Maries by the D38. Within 6km (4 miles), turn left on to the D85 and cross the Petit Rhône not by bridge but by the flat-bottomed ferry boat, which operates a free shuttle service across the river practically every ½ hour during summer (if you are in a hurry, then stay on the D38). The D85 is a quiet back road which gives you an even better chance of seeing the Camargue's wildlife. At the D58, turn left for the walled town of Aigues-Mortes.

3 Aigues-Mortes

Park your car outside the walls and walk through the main gate (still complete with its doors), the Porte de la Gardette. For the best view of the town, which is laid out in an orderly grid pattern, visit the Tour de Constance (Constance Tower) and ramparts.

Le Grau-du-Roi, a bustling little port with

The distinctive white horses of Camargue

a good range of restaurants and gently shelving sandy beach, is along the D979 from Aigues-Mortes. Continue on the coast road to the nearby futuristic resort of La Grande-Motte. Return towards Aigues-Mortes by the inland route, then take the D979 north, turning right on to the N572 for Vauvert and Arles.

Horses and bulls

The Camargue's white horses come from a distinct breed of unknown origin. Together with the black bulls of the region, they are the mainstay of the local Camarguais culture. The horses, bulls and sheep are looked after by *gardians* (local herdsmen). These hardy, proud Camargue-style cowboys play an important role in maintaining the traditions of the area, often working from a simple windowless thatched dwelling known as a *cabane*. The *gardians* are prominent figures in the summer festivals involving bulls and horses. Many towns and villages hold Provençal-style bullfights, in which the bull survives (always check beforehand to confirm details).

Cassis

This is where the Côte d'Azur unofficially begins. Cassis, 22km (14 miles) east of Marseille, is at the start of the most exotic, expensive stretch of coastline in Europe. The little resort, by Riviera standards, is understated and unpretentious, though its flower-bedecked streets are as impossibly busy during high summer as everywhere else along the coast.

Visitors come to Cassis for its three small beaches, picturesque harbour and idyllic location along a deep, mountain-backed bay. To appreciate this setting to the full, take the spectacular D141 coast road (the route des Crêtes) to La Ciotat and stop off at heart-stopping **Cap Canaille** – at around 400m (1,312ft), reputedly the highest cliff in continental Europe – which looks down directly into the clear blue-green waters of the bay.

Exploring the inaccessible coastline between Marseille and Cassis is not so easy. This strange, fjord-like shore, known as Les Calanques (*see box*), can be viewed by boat from Cassis's harbour.

La Ciotat

Whereas neighbouring Cassis is tucked snugly into its bay, La Ciotat sprawls lazily along a much more open coastline. La Ciotat is a resort of two halves: the old port, sheltering in the lee of Cap de l'Aigle, and a long sandy beach. The old port might not fulfil everyone's expectations. It still displays all the hallmarks of an unglamorous shipbuilding past, though some may find such an intrusion of down-to-earth reality refreshing on a coastline that assiduously courts a gilded image.

Beyond the café-lined harbour there lies an old town of considerable interest.

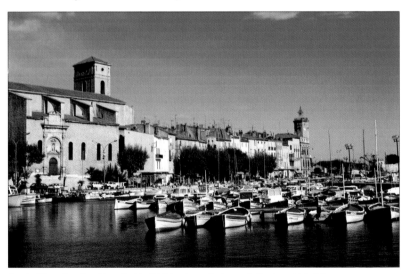

Fine buildings line the old port of La Ciotat, a town that once thrived on shipbuilding

Notre-Dame-de-l'Assomption is a grand 17th-century church overlooking the port, and there are chapels dedicated to the Blue and Black Penitents (*see p59*). History of a more contemporary kind was made in the beach district in 1895, with the first showing of motion pictures by the Lumière brothers.

Musée Ciotaden

This local museum traces the history of the town from ancient times, when it was an outpost of Marseille.
Ancien Hôtel de Ville, quai Ganteaume. Tel: 04 42 71 40 99; www.museeciotaden.org. Open: summer, Wed–Sun, 4–7pm; winter, Wed–Sun, 3–6pm. Admission charge.

La Ciotat is on the D559 between Marseille and Toulon.

Fontvieille

Forever associated with this small town at the western approach to the Alpilles is the writer Alphonse Daudet (1840–97). His mainly cheerful, ironic stories make him one of the most important humorists of his time, but his writing also reflected themes critical of society. Although Daudet's *Lettres de Mon Moulin* (*Letters from my Windmill*) were mostly composed in Paris, they were inspired by this locality. The windmill just south of the town contains a small museum dedicated to him. It stands on a summit that commands an excellent panorama northwards to the vast plain of the Rhône and eastwards to the angular Alpilles. At the foot of the hill there are more Daudet associations – in a museum in the **Château de**

Rugged and remote, the coastline between Marseille and Cassis is best explored by boat

Montauban, where Daudet often stayed. (A joint ticket gives admission to the mill and château – details from the Office de Tourisme, *tel: 04 90 54 67 49*.)

Also of interest in this area are the relatively unknown Roman remains a few kilometres south of Fontvieille. The **Aqueducs de Barbegal** are an impressive sight. A long line of ruined archways marks the route of the aqueduct, built to supply Arles with water from Eygalières, 50km (31 miles) away. The remains of a large 4th-century flour mill can also be seen.
Fontvieille is on the D17 about 10km (6 miles) northeast of Arles.

Les Calanques

This is the name given to the deeply indented limestone shoreline between Marseille and Cassis, a protected area and haven for wildlife. Arid, rugged and remote, Les Calanques are best explored by boat from Cassis. Calanque de Port-Miou and Calanque de Port-Pin (also accessible by footpath from a signposted car park west of Cassis) are the closest of this series of jutting, jagged inlets. The most memorable is the remoter Calanque d'En-Vau, where towering white cliffs plunge precipitously into the sea.

Marseille

Marseille, more famous for its association with crime, racism and the *French Connection* films than its ancient roots, is often bypassed by visitors. Yet it is one of France's largest cities and the capital of Provence. As such, it has a vitality, as well as an ancestry, that demands attention.

The many-domed Cathédrale de la Major

Very little remains of the Greek harbour colony of Massalia, founded in the 6th century BC. From Roman maritime base to the docklands and refineries of the 19th and 20th centuries, it has always been the port that has determined Marseille's cosmopolitan personality. The Vieux Port is as sunny and animated as any southern city. Leading from the quayside is the famous La Canebière, lined with cafés and shops.

Basilique de Notre-Dame-de-la-Garde

The steep climb to this 19th-century Romano-Byzantine church is worth it for the wonderful panoramas alone. *On an outcrop high above the port; head uphill and pick up the boulevard André Aune off rue/boulevard Fort Notre-Dame running from the quay.*

Abbaye de St-Victor

Marseille's oldest church has a crypt containing a 5th-century sepulchre. *Place St-Victor.*

Cathédrale de la Major

The giant 19th-century neo-Byzantine cathedral dwarfs its ancient harbinger, the Romanesque Major Ancienne. *Along avenue Robert Schuman.*

Château d'If

This craggy island-fortress, like San Francisco's Alcatraz, was used as a

Fort St-Nicolas is one of two forts (the other is St-Jean) guarding the harbour entrance prison for centuries (Edmond Dantés, hero of Alexander Dumas's *The Count of Monte Cristo*, was incarcerated here). *Visits by boat from quai des Belges. Tel: 04 91 55 50 09. Open: Tue–Sun, summer 9.30am–5pm; winter 9.30am–4pm. Admission charge.*

Musée des Beaux-Arts (Museum of Fine Arts)

Art from the 16th to 19th centuries is displayed here. *Palais Longchamp. Tel: 04 91 14 59 30. Open: summer, Tue–Sun, 11am–6pm; winter, Tue–Sun, 10am–5pm. Admission charge, except on Sun morning.*

Musée Cantini

20th-century paintings and sculptures. *19 rue Grignan. Tel: 04 91 54 77 75. Open: summer, Tue–Sun, 11am–6pm; winter, Tue–Sun, 10am–5pm. Admission charge.*

Musée des Docks Romains

The museum contains remains of a rare Roman warehouse plus other artefacts. *Place Vivaux. Tel: 04 91 91 24 62. Open: summer, Tue–Sun, 11am–6pm; winter, Tue–Sun, 10am–5pm. Admission charge.*

Musée d'Histoire de Marseille

Covering prehistory to the Gallo-Roman period, the most famous exhibit here is a freeze-dried Roman merchant vessel. *Centre Bourse. Tel: 04 91 90 42 22. Open: Mon–Sat, noon–7pm. Admission charge.*

Musée du Vieux Marseille Maison Diamantée

This museum of social history is based at the 16th-century Maison Diamantée –

Brass plaque on the quai des Belges dedicated to the Marseille poet Victor Gelu

so called for the diamond shaped stones that characterise its façade. *2 rue de la Prison. Tel: 04 91 55 28 68. Open: summer, Tue–Sun, 11am–6pm; winter, Tue–Sun, 10am–5pm. Admission charge.*

Musée Grobet-Labadié

Once the private property of Louis Grobet and Marie-Louise Labadié, this museum displays their extensive collection of furniture, ceramics, paintings and tapestries. *140 boulevard Longchamp. Tel: 04 91 62 21 82. Open: summer, Tue–Sun, 11am–6pm; winter, Tue–Sun, 10am–5pm. Admission charge.*

La Vieille Charité

A restored 17th-century hospice, designed by Pierre Puget, Vieille Charité's contemporary role is as a centre for the arts and science. Exhibitions and special events are held here, and it is home to the excellent **Musée d'Archéologie Méditerranéenne**. *2 rue de la Charité. Tel: 04 91 14 58 58. Open: summer, daily, 11am–6pm; winter, daily, 10am–5pm. Admission charge.*

Walk: Marseille

Marseille is a big city, but don't be intimidated by the flyovers, factories and urban sprawl on the approach. This is a city which walkers can quite easily get to grips with (after finding a place to park!), for most of the interest lies around the Vieux Port (Old Port). The Vieux Port is Marseille's birthplace and remains its vibrant heart. Belying the images of a dark-alleyed, slightly sinister city riddled with crime, this part of Marseille is inherently Mediterranean, colourful, and exceedingly photogenic.

Allow a day for the walk.

From the Office de Tourisme at 4 La Canebière, walk down to quai des Belges.

1 Quai des Belges

Quai des Belges looks out across the Vieux Port, which was discovered by the Phoenicians in 600 BC. Tiered, pastel-shaded houses and grand buildings line the quayside, which is the venue for the morning fish market. Overlooking the large harbour, which bristles with a forest of yacht masts, is the enormous neo-Byzantine Basilique de Notre-Dame-de-la-Garde, standing on a 162-m (531-ft) high limestone outcrop.

Quai du Port leads to the handsome **Hôtel de Ville**, a fine example of 17th-century baroque Provençal architecture. *Turn right here along rue de la Prison for the Musée du Vieux Marseille (Museum of Old Marseille) housed in the 16th-century Maison Diamantée. Close by, along rue du Lacydon at place Vivaux, is the Musée des Docks Romains.*

Retrace your steps a short way along rue de Lacydon and climb the steps to rue Caisserie, crossing the road to climb a much narrower, historic staircase, montée des Accoules.

2 Montée des Accoules

Montée des Accoules takes you into Le Panier, the oldest part of Marseille. Much of Le Panier was destroyed by the Nazis during World War II. On the hilly slopes above the Vieux Port, the surviving section – a rabbit warren of claustrophobic, narrow streets and alleyways hemmed in by tall buildings – preserves an authentic atmosphere of Marseille as it once was.

Montée des Accoules leads to place de Lenche, where you turn right along rue de l'Évêché, then left along rue Four du Chapitre towards the waterfront and the Cathédrale de la Major. Proceed along avenue Robert Schuman, turning right into rue Antoine-Becker, left along rue de l'Évêché, right into place Francis Chirat, and right again into rue de l'Observance. The large building on your left is la Vieille Charité (Old Charity Cultural Centre), the entrance to which is off rue de la Charité (turn left at the end of rue de l'Observance).

From rue de la Charité turn right into rue Puits du Denier, then left into rue du Panier. Rue des Moulins leads to the pleasant, tree-lined place des Moulins, and on to montée des Accoules. Walk back down the steps, turning left into rue Caisserie, then on to Grand Rue, crossing over rue de la République – one of the city's main streets – to the Jardin des Vestiges (Garden of Ruins).

3 Jardin des Vestiges

You can take a well-earned rest in this attractive sunken garden, excavated to reveal the fortifications of the original Greek town that existed here, Massalia, the 1st-century docks and the 3rd-century entranceway.

The **Musée d'Histoire de Marseille** (open: Mon–Sat, 12–7pm) is located here, part of the huge Centre Bourse shopping complex.

From the garden, follow rue Henri Barbusse to rue Reine Élisabeth, cross La Canebière, then keep on rue Paradis till it crosses rue Arignan. Musée Cantini will be on your left.

Marseille

Nîmes

Denim originated in the textile mills of Nîmes (*de Nîmes*: denim). Despite the ubiquity of the cloth, the city is more famous as a place of great antiquity, exemplified by its outstandingly well-preserved Arènes (Roman amphitheatre). In recent years Nîmes has attracted much attention for its bold – and sometimes controversial – experiments in urban regeneration with futuristic buildings such as the Carrée d'Art. While there is still some way to go (parts of the city are still in need of care and attention), Nîmes has become a fascinating place for lovers of architecture and art old and new.

The ruins of the Roman Amphitheatre are still in use

Arènes (Roman Amphitheatre)

This vast amphitheatre, dating from the 1st century and one of the best preserved in the whole of the Roman world, is still in regular use for everything from pop concerts to bullfights. Its two-storey façade encloses a complex building of galleries, vaulted passageways and tiered terraces that can accommodate over 20,000 people. Other Roman sites in Nîmes include the **Porte Auguste** (Augustus's Gate) and

The Maison Carrée: a rectangular temple in Greek style by the Romans

Castellum (a water tower), a short distance northeast and northwest of the centre respectively.
Boulevard des Arènes. Tel: 04 66 21 82 56. Open: summer, daily, 9.30am–6.30pm; winter, daily, 10am–5pm. Closed: during public events. Admission charge.

Cathédrale Notre-Dame et St-Castor

Although dating from 1096, it has been almost totally remodelled and rebuilt over the centuries. Note the preserved frieze in the west front, which depicts scenes from the Old Testament.
Place aux Herbes.

Jardin de la Fontaine

This delightful garden is, for many, the highlight of their visit to Nîmes. Created in 1750 around the spring that gave Nîmes its existence, it is France's first public garden, set against a backdrop of rocky, wooded slopes. On the slopes above stands the **Tour Magne**, a 34-m (112-ft) high Roman tower

Place aux Herbes, which contains the former bishop's palace, now a museum

commanding spectacular views.
Northwest of city centre. Open: Gardens summer, daily, 9am–7pm; winter, daily, 9.30am–6pm. Tour Magne: daily, 9.30am–12.30pm & 1.30–4.30pm. Admission charge, free admission to gardens.

Maison Carrée

This colonnaded Roman temple ('The Square House') is unique for its state of preservation, which belies its age of nearly 2,000 years. Neat and, in spite of its name, rectangular, its purity of line and harmonious proportions have given it a reputation as one of the finest temples in the Greek tradition outside Italy. Its interior is currently used to display works of art.
Place de la Maison Carrée. Tel: 04 66 21 82 56. Open: daily, 9.30am–12.30pm & 1.30–4.30pm. Free admission.

Musée Archéologique

If you want to feast your eyes on Roman artefacts, then this is the place to visit.

The **Musée d'Histoire Naturelle et de Préhistoire** (Museum of Natural History and Prehistory – *tel: 04 66 67 39 14*) is housed at the same address.
13 bis boulevard Amiral-Courbet. Tel: 04 66 76 74 80. Open: summer, Tue–Sun, 10am–6pm; winter, Tue–Sun, 11am–6pm. Admission charge.

Musée des Beaux-Arts

The gallery has a large Roman mosaic, paintings of the French, Italian, Flemish and Dutch schools from the 15th to mid-19th centuries, and modern art.
Rue de la Cité Foulc. Tel: 04 66 67 38 21. Open: Tue–Sun 10am–6pm (Thur 12–8pm). Admission charge.

Musée du Vieux Nîmes (Museum of Old Nîmes)

The museum contains an interesting selection of Provençal and Languedocian furniture, pottery, painting and everyday objects.
Place aux Herbes. Tel: 04 66 76 73 70. Open: Tue–Sun 10am–6pm. Free admission.

Walk: Nîmes

Nîmes has an unexpected variety of faces – part elegant, part shabby, part historic, part futuristic. The ancient heart of the city, a maze of narrow streets and passageways, is ringed by wide and busy roads – boulevard Victor-Hugo, boulevard Gambetta, boulevard de la Libération and boulevard Amiral Courbet. The creation of a conservation zone in 1985 has led to the refurbishment of old Nîmes. Conveniently for those on foot, most of the main sites are concentrated in and around this central area (the beautiful Jardin de la Fontaine, some distance northwest of the centre, is one of the few exceptions).

Allow at least half a day for the walk.

From the Office de Tourisme at 6 rue Auguste, walk a short distance south to the Maison Carrée.

1 Maison Carrée

Along with the Arènes (Roman amphitheatre), this Roman temple is Nîmes' most famous landmark. Across the open space from Maison Carrée lies an architectural counterpoint in the form of a new – and controversial – building of typically bold, uncompromising design. This is the **Carré d'Art** (Art Cube – *tel: 04 66 76 35 70; open: Tue–Sun, 10am–6pm*), the work of British architect Sir Norman Foster. Intended as a Pompidou Centre of the south, it serves as an art gallery and library.

Walk south along boulevard Victor-Hugo, visiting Église St-Paul, built in the 19th century in Romano-Byzantine style. Take rue de la Monnaie to place du Marché.

2 Place du Marché

Place du Marché is the scene of Nîmes' medieval corn market. The charming modern marble and bronze fountain with a crocodile echoes the city's crest. *Leave the place by rue Fresque, a road lined with historic houses. Turn right into rue de Bernis and right again along rue de l'Aspic, a busy shopping street. Turn left into rue de l'Hôtel de Ville. The 15th-century archway beside the Hôtel de Ville leads to rue de la Trésorerie. Turn right into rue Dorée, another street lined with historic but dilapidated houses. At Grand Rue, turn left.*

3 Chapelle des Jésuites

The 17th-century former Jesuit Chapel along Grand Rue is one of a number of sites in Nîmes that demonstrate the imaginative, forward-thinking attitude of the city authorities. It is now used for cultural events, and in summer its cool,

spacious interior becomes an exhibition area for works of modern art.
Turn left into rue du Chapitre.

4 Hôtel de Régis

The Hôtel de Régis at 14 rue du Chapitre is another of the city's many fine old dwellings. An 18th-century façade with a carved entranceway leads into a magnificent cobbled courtyard (16th-century) with Roman artefacts.
Turn right along rue des Marchands for the pretty place aux Herbes and the Cathédrale Notre-Dame et St-Castor, together with its neighbour, the Musée du Vieux Nîmes. Along rue de la Madeleine,

take a short detour down rue Ste-Eugénie to see the Église Ste-Eugénie, the oldest church in the city. From rue de la Madeleine, turn left into rue de l'Aspic, which leads south to the Arènes (Roman amphitheatre).

5 Esplanade Charles de Gaulle

The Esplanade beyond the Arènes is a pleasant place to end the walk. Its 1848 **Fontaine Pradier** (named after its sculptor) depicts a female figure who symbolises Nîmes. The grand **Palais de Justice** (Law Courts), in neoclassical style, stands on one side of the Esplanade.

Nîmes

Pont du Gard

This 275-m (902-ft) long
Roman aqueduct was
constructed in the 1st
century to span the
Gardon Valley. It was the
crowning glory of a 50-km
(31-mile) system of
tunnels, ditches, water-
regulating basins and other
bridges, built to carry
water from Uzès to Nîmes.
The construction of the
Pont du Gard represented
a truly monumental feat of
engineering. Giant blocks
of dressed stone were
hoisted and then slotted
into place without mortar.
Built in three tiers, it has
35 arches along the top
directly below the water
channel – still visible
where covering stones are
missing – 11 arches in the
middle, and six at the
bottom (surprisingly, only
one of these bottom arches
actually spans the river).
The structure towers
nearly 50m (164 ft) above
the waters of the Gardon,
yet possesses a sense of
harmony that modern
bridge builders seem
incapable of replicating.
A road built in the 17th
century along the east side
of the bottom tier carries
traffic, forming part of the
minor road D981. But the
Pont du Gard's really
miraculous feature is its
state of preservation. Its
weathered golden
stonework looks good for
another 2,000 years, and
you get the impression that

The fountain near the Porte de l'Horloge in Salon-de-Provence sports
a mossy coat

NOSTRADAMUS
1503–1566

Nostradamus was
born Michel de
Nostre Dame in St-Rémy –
to Jewish parents. As with
most Jews in southern
France, they had been
forced by the Inquisition
to espouse the Catholic
faith. As a student, he
devoted much time to
languages and science,
attending the University
of Avignon, where he
studied liberal arts, and
the University of
Montpellier, where he
qualified as a doctor.

Nostradamus lost his
first wife and two children
to the plague – despite
having found a remedy
for the disease – and,
distraught, he travelled
France and Italy for six
years. In 1554 he settled
in Salon-de-Provence and
remarried. Over the years
he garnered a reputation
as something of a
prophet and wrote his
famous Les Centuries, a
series of theses and
predictions. A decade
later he was appointed
Royal Physician to
Charles IX and two years
later died in his sleep.

the bridge could be returned to full working order in a few days.

Increasing numbers of visitors threaten the conservation of this important site. To raise awareness of the bridge's illustrious past, an interesting information centre-cum-museum has been structured outlining its history, and explaining the aqueduct's route and function, and includes a section of exhibits as well as a short film designed with children in mind. The parkland grounds, strewn with Roman remains, prove popular for picnics. The whole area is accessible free of charge but the car park has fixed opening hours.
Tel: 08 20 90 33 30.
Parking open: summer 9.30am–7pm; rest of the year till 6pm.
Admission charge for parking.

Salon-de-Provence

Salon's medieval centre, huddling beneath a rocky hill crowned by the Château de l'Empéri, has seen quite a few changes of late. French architects and town planners have been mostly successful in rejuvenating the heart of the town. New apartments rub shoulders with renovated 16th-century houses, smart shops are beginning to appear in the maze of old streets, and the 13th-century Église St-Michel is having a face-lift. Mercifully, Salon has not been emasculated by this modern development, save at the foot of the château in the place des Centuries, a hopeless open space devoid of life.

Forgetting this one sad mistake, Salon has much to delight the eye. The 18th-century mossy fountain outside the Porte de l'Horloge gateway

resembles a giant green toadstool. Along the rue de l'Horloge there is a huge, attention-grabbing mural featuring Michel de Nostradamus (1503–66), the physician/astrologer who spent the last 19 years of his life here. A statue to another famous resident – civil engineer Adam de Craponne (1527–76), whose canal brought water to this previously arid region – stands outside the splendid 17th-century Hôtel de Ville (Town Hall).

Château/Musée de l'Empéri

A military museum of the French armies from Louis XIV to 1914 is housed in the massive castle.
Tel: 04 90 56 22 36. Open: daily, 10am–noon & 2–6pm. Admission charge.

Musée Grevin de la Provence

The history and legends of Provence are imaginatively presented here.
Place des Centuries. Tel: 04 90 56 36 30. Open: 9am–noon & 2–6pm. Closed: Sat & Sun morning. Admission charge.

Musée de Nostradamus

A museum devoted to his work in the house where this fascinating man lived.
11 rue Nostradamus. Tel: 04 90 56 64 31. Open: as for Musée Grevin. Admission charge.

Musée du Savon et de Marseille

A historical journey into the origins of Provence's famous Marseille soap.
148 ave Paul-Bourret. Tel: 04 90 53 24 77; www.marius-fabre.fr. Open: Mon–Fri, 9.30–11.30am & 2–5pm (until 4pm on Fri). Admission charge.
Salon-de-Provence is 53km (33 miles) northwest of Marseille.

Les Antiques near St-Rémy-de-Provence: detail on the Roman triumphal arch

St-Rémy-de-Provence

St-Rémy is another famous Roman town. Les Antiques – a generic name covering St-Rémy's outstanding commemorative arch and mausoleum – stand side by side a short distance south of the town on the D5 to Les Baux. The arch signalled the entrance to Glanum, an excavated, mainly Roman, settlement, one of the most significant ancient sites in France.

The historic centre of St-Rémy itself is compact, charming and self-contained. Nostradamus, whose predictions have intrigued people for centuries, was born along rue Hoche in 1503. Vincent Van Gogh's time in St-Rémy is remembered in the Centre d'Art in the **Hôtel Estrine**. During his 12-month stay at the St-Paul-de-Mausole psychiatric clinic near Les Antiques, he painted around 150 canvases, including some of his most famous paintings, such as *The Starry Night* and *Wheat Field with Cypress*. The building, originally a 12th-century monastery, is still a clinic.
8 rue Estrine. Church and cloisters open: mornings and afternoons. Free admission.

Les Antiques

Both monuments are located on the roadside. The triumphal arch is decorated with beautiful Greek-influenced carvings celebrating the Roman conquest of Marseille. Next to it is one of the world's best-preserved Roman structures, still standing at its full 18m (59 ft). Although it has always been known as a mausoleum, it is now thought to have been a monument to Lucius and Caius, grandsons of Augustus Caesar.
2km (1¹/4 miles) south of the town centre along avenue Vincent-Van-Gogh. Free admission.

Centre d'Art Présence Van Gogh

Changing exhibitions of modern works plus a permanent display of reproductions of Van Gogh's works can be seen in the beautiful 18th-century Hôtel Estrine.
8 rue Estrine. Tel: 04 90 92 34 72. Open: mid-Mar–mid-Oct, Tue–Sun, 10am–1pm & 3–7pm; mid-Oct–Dec, Tue–Sun, 10.30am–12.30pm & 2–6pm. Admission charge.

Glanum

When Glanum was excavated from 1921 onwards, it revealed evidence of Neolithic settlement. Later, in the 2nd century BC, a Gallo-Greek town was established here. But what we see today is mainly Roman, more or less spanning the 1st to 3rd centuries AD. Glanum was an army base, spa town and important crossroads for two major routes between Italy and Spain. The extensive ruins provide a wonderful insight into the life of a thriving Roman city. There are houses,

monuments, temples, columns, a forum, canal, fortified gateway, swimming pool, thermal baths and spring.
2km (1¹/₄ miles) south of the town centre along avenue Vincent-Van-Gogh.
Tel: 04 90 92 23 79. Open: Apr–Aug, daily, 10am–6.30pm; Sept–Mar, daily, 10.30am–5pm. Admission charge.

Musée des Alpilles

Well-presented displays focus mainly on folk culture, crafts and local traditions.
Place Favier. Tel: 04 90 92 68 24.
Open: Jan–Feb & Nov–Dec, Tue–Sat, 2–5pm; Mar–June & Sept–Oct, Tue–Sat, 10am–noon & 2–6pm; July–Aug, Tue–Sat, 10am–12.30pm & 2–7pm.
Admission charge.

Musée Archéologique

Glanum's excavated artefacts are exhibited here.
Place Favier. Tel: 04 90 92 64 04. Open: as for archaeological site. Admission charge.
St-Rémy-de-Provence is 40km (25 miles) northwest of Salon-de-Provence.

Tarascon

This town on the banks of the Rhône boasts a splendid fairy-tale castle, the

> ### Good King René
>
> A scholar and artist, 'le bon roi' René d'Anjou ruled Provence from its capital, Aix, and his impregnable castle at Tarascon. After losing Anjou to the King of France, he settled in Provence in 1434, dying 44 years later in 1480. He was king in name only of Hungary, Jerusalem and Naples. His rule in Provence was a period of great cultural expansion. René's father, Louis II d'Anjou, had founded the University of Aix and in his mould René continued nurturing an interest in the arts and in true Renaissance style encouraged their patronage.

Château du Roi René. This is one of the best-preserved 15th-century castles in France. It rises above the waters of the Rhône to face yet another stirring castle at Beaucaire on the opposite bank.

Château du Roi René

Impregnable defences protect a surprisingly decorative and luxurious interior.
Boulevard du Roi René. Tel: 04 90 91 01 93. Open: daily, Apr–Sept 9am–7pm; Oct–Mar Tue–Sun 10.30am–5pm. Admission charge.

Tarascon is about 16km (10 miles) west of St-Rémy.

King René's majestic castle beside the River Rhône at Tarascon

Var

The Riviera proper starts within this *département*. Away from the main resort areas, the rugged coastlines fringing the forested Massif des Maures and Massif de l'Estérel still preserve their natural beauty. Inland, thickly wooded hills rise into the Haut-Var, a huge expanse of bare plateaux and deserted uplands.

One of the many pretty fountains in Aups

Aups

At an altitude of over 500m (1,640ft), Aups is traditionally regarded as the beginning of the Alps. Standing among the high plains and empty spaces of the Haut-Var, this peaceful little town preserves an authentic country atmosphere.

Markets are held on Wednesday and Saturday in the square beside the Hôtel de Ville (Town Hall). There is much to appreciate in Aups's unspoilt, leafy old streets: the many fountains, the impressive Renaissance portal and renovated doorway to the Église St-Pancrace, the remains of a town gate and ramparts at the far end of rue des Aires.

Musée Simon Segal

This small gallery displays works by Russian-born painter Simon Segal and other modern artists.
Avenue Albert-1er. Tel: 04 94 70 01 95. Open: July–Aug, Wed–Mon, 10am–noon & 4–7pm. Admission charge.

Bandol, with its marina, casino and elegant villas is the epitome of Côte d'Azur style

Var

Aups is 29km (18 miles) north of Draguignan.

Bandol

Bandol has all the attributes of a stylish Côte d'Azur resort: the palm trees, the beaches, the casino, the marina, the expensive villas and condominiums. The resort has another asset – the **Île de Bendor**, a short distance offshore, owned by *pastis* magnate Paul Ricard. The small island, accessible by a frequent boat service, contains a diving school, arts and conference centres, and a museum dedicated to wines and spirits.

Bandol's neighbouring resort **Sanary-sur-Mer** also offers boat trips – in this case, to the larger **Île des Embiez**.

Jardin Exotique et Zoo

This tropical garden and zoo is a popular attraction.
Located near the autoroute exit for Bandol. Tel: 04 94 29 40 38; www.zoosanary.com. Open: daily, 8am–noon & 2–7pm (until 6pm in winter). Closed: Sun mornings in winter. Admission charge.

Bandol is about 16km (10 miles) west of Toulon.

View of the old town, Bormes-les-Mimosas

Bormes-les-Mimosas

You can forgive the locals for embellishing the name of this hilltop village, originally known simply as Bormes and rechristened Bormes-les-Mimosas in 1968. There are flowers everywhere, in baskets, urns, tubs, pots and window boxes, climbing up the fronts of the houses, and in immaculately tended flowerbeds.

The part of Bormes that attracts visitors – the Vieux Village (Old Village) – is perched at the top of a steep, south-facing slope, with wonderful views of nearby Le Lavandou and the coast. The alleyways and narrow streets can be explored by following a waymarked Circuit Touristique with numbered stopping-off places (details from the tourist office, *tel: 04 94 01 38 38*). Bormes is almost too perfect: the street

names are a little fanciful – montée du Paradis, for instance – and there are even special slatted cubbyholes in which to hide the dustbins!

Musée d'Art et Histoire

Bormes's history together with the work of local artist Jean-Charles Cazin (1841–1901) are the main themes here. *65 rue Carnot. Tel: 04 94 71 56 60. Open: Tue–Sat, 10am–noon & 2.30–5pm, Sun, 10am–noon. Admission charge.*

Bormes-les-Mimosas is off the D559 about 22km (14 miles) east of Hyères.

Draguignan

This large town stands at the gateway to the high country of the Haut-Var. There is not a great deal to distract visitors passing through on the way to the

Grand Cañon du Verdon. The most attractive part of the town is the medieval quarter around the place du Marché, the Tour de l'Horloge (a fine 17th-century clock tower) and the Église St-Michel, guarded by ancient gateways.

Musée des Arts et Traditions Populaires

Exhibits include traditional costumes, agricultural implements and a Provençal kitchen.

15 rue Joseph-Roumanille.
Tel: 04 94 47 05 72. Open: 9am–noon &
2–6pm. Closed Sun morning & Mon.
Admission charge.

Draguignan is 30km (19 miles) northwest of Fréjus.

Fréjus/St Raphaël

Fréjus is a place of many parts, and blends into its more fashionable neighbour, St-Raphaël. Most visitors come for the beach, **Fréjus-Plage**, at the western end of this sprawling coastal town. In the east there is a smart new marina and harbour complex, while beyond that a long, sandy beach ends at St Raphaël's attractive harbour and seafront casino.

The town of Fréjus itself, 1km (^{2}/$_3$ mile) or so inland, is noted for its Roman remains. **Forum Julii** was a large Roman town and port: too large, perhaps, for us to appreciate fully today, since vestiges of Roman occupation are scattered across a wide area, making it difficult to build up any coherent

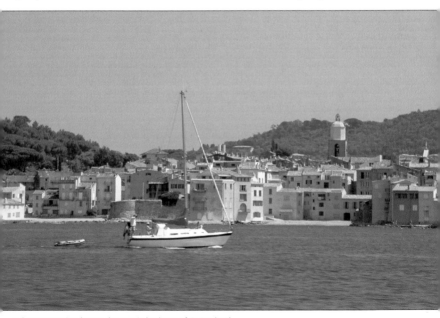

A boat excursion leaves the scenic harbour of St Raphaël

Popular since the 19th century, Hyères is more of a genuine town than many other resorts

picture. Beside the N7 into town from the northeast are ruined arches from a 40-km (25-mile) aqueduct system. An open-air theatre (still used for concerts) stands incongruously amongst quiet suburbs along avenue du Théâtre-Romain, while the Arènes (amphitheatre) lies beyond the Porte des Gaules gateway in the west of the town. Medieval Fréjus's centrepiece is the Cathedral Close, a collection of important religious buildings dating back to early Christian times.

Arènes (Amphitheatre)
Although not as impressive as others in Provence, it is still used for concerts and bullfights.
Rue Henri-Vadon. Tel: 04 94 51 34 31. Open: winter, Tue–Sun, 9.30am–12.30pm & 2–5pm; summer, Tue–Sun,

9.30am–12.30pm & 2–6pm. Admission charge.

Cathedral Close
The well-preserved baptistery here is one of the oldest in France. It stands next to an impressive 10th- to 13th-century cathedral built in an austere early Provençal style. Lighter in effect are its slender-columned cloisters, enclosing a delightful little garden. An archaeological museum is also located here.
Place Formigé. Tel: 04 94 51 26 30. Cathedral open: mornings & 2.30–6.30pm. Free admission. Baptistery, cloisters and museum open: winter, Tue–Sun, 9am–noon & 2–5pm; summer, daily, 9am–6.30pm. Admission charge. Fréjus is 37km (23 miles) north of St-Tropez.

Hyères
Miraculously, the town of Hyères has avoided the worst excesses of Côte tourism, possibly because of its location a short distance inland (the coast has receded since medieval times, when Hyères served as a port for the Crusades). Even the 'new' Hyères of the 19th century, which covers the hill on the approach to the old town, has preserved its original decorum. This area, with its wide streets, waving palm trees, gardens, grand villas and casino, retains the character of its *belle époque* when it rivalled Nice as a fashionable resort for the rich and famous (Queen Victoria stayed here once).

The Vieille Ville of medieval Hyères lies beyond the ancient gateway at place Georges-Clémenceau. Suddenly, you are amongst the narrow, typically claustrophobic streets of a real French town in which real people live and work. Old Hyères has not been cosmeticised with overly pretty features and overtly expensive shops – and is all the more refreshing for it. Place Massillon, venue of a daily market, is a delightful little self-contained Provençal square surrounded by tall buildings and unglamorous cafés. It is overlooked by the Tour St-Blaise, a 12th-century tower of the Knights Templar.

The Vieille Ville's main church, the imposing 13th-century Église St-Louis, is on place de la République east of place Massillon. Hyères's most memorable religious site stands high on the hill in place St-Paul. **Collégiale St-Paul** is a former collegiate church attached by archway to a Renaissance house with a fairy-tale conical turret (the Romanesque church is open afternoons, except Monday). Place St-Paul, a magnificent viewpoint 5km (3 miles)

from the sea, looks out past the narrow spit of land known as Presqu'île de Giens to the Îles d'Hyères. If you have the energy, you can climb yet further up the hill to the flower-filled Parc St-Bernard and a ruined château.

Hyères' beaches lie to the south, along Hyères-Plage and the 5-km (3-mile) long Presqu'île de Giens.

Jardin Olbius-Riquier

This attractive garden, south of the town, contains a lake, children's play area, aviaries, a profusion of exotic plants and a small zoo.

Avenue Ambroise-Thomas. Open: daily, 7.30am–dusk. Free admission.

Site Olbia

Greek and Roman finds from local excavations are on display, together with paintings and items of natural history.

Open: Tue & Sat, 3–6.30pm, Thur & Fri, 9.30am–12.30pm & 3–6.30pm. Admission charge.

Sea, sand and sunshine at Le Lavandou – but expect high prices in the town

Îles d'Hyères

Boats for the islands of Porquerolles, Port-Cros and Le Levant – also known as the Îles d'Or (Golden Isles) – depart daily all year round from Port d'Hyères, next to Hyères-Plage. A few kilometres east of Hyères, **La Londe-les-Maures/Port-de-Miramar** has daily boat trips from mid-June to mid-September. One-way journeys last from 30–90 minutes depending on port of departure, with shorter times from La Londe.

The nearest and largest of these islands, Porquerolles, is predictably the most developed, though everything is on a small scale. You can walk or cycle (bikes can be rented locally) through a landscape of pine trees, eucalyptus and heather to some beautiful sandy beaches and stunning stretches of cliff scenery. Fort Ste-Agathe, a stronghold over-looking the village, has a small museum. The Île de Port-Cros, more or less uninhabited, is a thickly vegetated haven that supports a wealth of wildlife. The smallest national park in France, this is the place to go for those interested in natural history. The Île du Levant, the furthest of the three islands from Hyères, is mainly a military base.
Office de Tourisme, Forum du Casino, 3 ave Ambroise Thomas, 83400 Hyères Cedex; tel: 04 94 01 84 50.

Le Lavandou

Travelling eastwards along the coast, you will begin to sense the presence of first-division glamour – and serious money – on reaching Le Lavandou. This is another fishing village that has become a glittering haven for holiday yachts. Not as densely developed as many of its contemporaries, it boasts a fine, spacious sandy beach and an animated harbour. Boats leave from the harbour for the Îles d'Hyères. The coast road east winds its way along the mountain-backed Corniche des Maures to St-Tropez. *Le Lavandou is 23km (14 1/4 miles) east of Hyères.*

St-Tropez

There are those who say that St-Tropez is impossible and over-hyped. And they are probably correct if they are referring to the resort in high summer. But come in the quieter months, and you immediately appreciate why St-Tropez has cast a spell over so many, from Matisse to Brigitte Bardot.

After such heightened expectations, St-Tropez's diminutive size comes as quite a surprise. The Vieux Port (Old Port) is the heart of St-Tropez. It is here that the multi-millionaires moor their huge yachts. It is here that the merely rich come to parade. And it is here that the *petit bourgeoisie* come to gawp at the ostentatious displays of wealth.

Behind the Vieux Port lies a picturesque town and the rue de la Citadelle, which leads to a high bluff dominated by a mighty 16th-century fortress.

St-Tropez's beach area lies a few kilometres to the south. The **Plage de Pampelonne**, although it has 5km (3 miles) of sand, becomes exceedingly busy in summer. Further south again, around Cape Camarat, there is a better chance of finding a quieter spot along the Plage de l'Escalet.

At the approach to the St-Tropez peninsula is **Port Grimaud**. Reclaimed from marshland in the 1960s, it is a

The jet set

The Riviera has long been a playground of the wealthy, the very name conjuring up images of 24-carat lifestyles involving luxury yachts, palatial hotels, bougainvillaea-draped villas, private beaches and spinning roulette wheels.

It was not always so. When the English novelist Tobias Smollett sought a cure for his bronchitis in Nice in 1764, he wrote of a land of 'rude peasants and persistent mosquitoes', though he did find the climate to his taste. Another Englishman, Lord Brougham – the Lord Chancellor, no less – found it even more to his liking 90 years later, when an enforced stay in the tiny fishing village of Cannes proved far more agreeable than he had expected. Within a decade, so many of his compatriots were travelling south for the winter that Nice had a Promenade des Anglais (Promenade of the English). By the end of the 19th century, the Riviera was playing host to Queen Victoria and the crowned heads of Italy, Sweden, Bulgaria and Belgium, as well as Grand Dukes of Russia and the Shah of Persia. 'Princes, princes, nothing but princes,' grumbled that master of the short story, Guy de Maupassant.

The clientele changed with the social upheaval that followed World War I. Newly rich Americans swarmed in with their taste for high living, making the Riviera a symbol of the Jazz Age. It was here that Gabrielle 'Coco' Chanel – perfumer and fashion designer – made sunbathing chic, and nowhere did the Roaring Twenties roar more excitingly. The area's seal of fashionable approval was again renewed when film star Grace Kelly came here to marry Prince Rainier.

Today the Côte d'Azur is as siren-like as ever, despite the dangers of being swamped by its own success. Movie stars, millionaires, pop singers, successful writers – all fall victim to the allure of sunshine, sybaritic living and the prestige that comes with being one of the jet set.

Antibes (above) and St Tropez are the playgrounds of the seriously rich. Princess Grace (left), an everlasting emblem of the Riviera

You have to go a few kilometres south from St-Tropez to enjoy the beaches

mostly successful attempt to create the look of a traditional fishing village in the modern idiom. Inland is the pretty hilltop village of **Grimaud**, capped by a ruined château.

La Citadelle et Musée Naval
The 16th-century fort is now a naval museum reflecting St-Tropez's maritime history.
Tel: 04 94 97 06 53. Open: Apr–June, daily, 10am–12.30pm & 1.30–6.30pm; July–Sept, daily, 10am–8pm; Oct–Mar, daily, 10am–12.30pm & 1.30–5.30pm. Admission charge.

Musée de l'Annonciade
This outstanding gallery contains the best selection of 1890–1950 paintings outside Paris: Braque, Dufy, Matisse, Signac, Utrillo and many others.
Place Grammont. Tel: 04 94 17 84 10.

Open: winter, Wed–Mon, 10am–noon & 2–6pm; spring, Wed–Mon, 10am–1pm & 3–9pm; summer, Wed–Mon, 10am–1pm & 3–10pm. Closed: Nov & second half of June. Admission charge.

Ste-Maxime
Ste-Maxime is an attractive, unpretentious resort. The seafront Office de Tourisme has a fascinating display of postcards depicting the Ste-Maxime of old.

Musée des Traditions Locales
Items of local folklore and traditions are housed in a 16th-century tower.
Tour Carrée. Tel: 04 94 96 70 30. Open: Wed–Sun, 10am–noon & 3–6pm (till 7pm in July). Admission charge.
Ste-Maxime is across the bay from St-Tropez.

Toulon

Capital of the Var and France's second-largest naval base, Toulon merits at least a mention in any guidebook to Provence. But it is mainly a large, modern and undistinguished city, with the exception of parts of the Vieille Ville (Old Town) behind quai Stalingrad and quai de la Sinse, an area that escaped the relentless bombings of World War II. North of the city, a cable car climbs to the summit of Mont Faron, from which you can appreciate Toulon's maritime appeal as a perfectly sheltered, capacious harbour.

Musée de la Marine

Toulon's long-standing associations with the sea are explained through model ships, drawings and memorabilia.
*Place Monsenergue. Tel: 04 94 02 02 01;
www.musee-marine.fr.*

*Open: summer, daily, 10am–6.30pm,
winter, Wed–Mon, 10am–noon & 2–6pm.
Admission charge.*

Musée d'Art and the Musée d'Histoire Naturelle

These two museums, with the same address, present two quite different collections. The former contains an excellent collection of paintings and sculptures spanning some 500 years. The latter offers exhibits of stuffed birds, mammals, mineral and botanical items that put the area into perspective.
*113 boulevard Leclerc.
Tel: 04 94 36 81 00.
Art Museum open: Tue–Sun, noon–6pm.
Natural History Museum open: Mon–Fri,
9am–6pm, Sat & Sun, 11am–6pm. Free
admission to both.
Toulon is 69km (43 miles) southwest of
St-Tropez.*

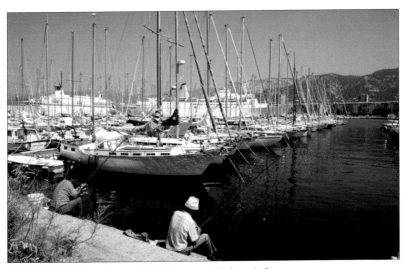

The naval base of Toulon has one of the finest natural harbours in France

Tour: L'Estérel

The Massif de l'Estérel, a mountain range which rises to over 600m (1,969ft), is the perfect antidote to the Côte d'Azur's curse of too many people and too much development. This wild, rugged and largely impenetrable upland, covered in *maquis* (scrub), a dense covering of heathers, gorse, mimosa, lavender and other shrubs, has a coastal equivalent along the indented Corniche de l'Estérel. Although just a stone's throw from Cannes, this is the least built-up stretch of coastline between Toulon and the Italian border, though how long it will remain so is open to question. On this tour, you will see a rash of new development, some of it clinging precariously to impossibly steep slopes in order to achieve that all-important sea view.

Allow a full day, including some time to stop off at the coast.

From Fréjus, take the coast road via the marina to St-Raphaël (see p81). On leaving St-Raphaël by the N98 coast road you will soon be amongst the rich red volcanic rocks, small coves and sand-and-pebble beaches that characterise the Corniche de l'Estérel (its nickname is the Corniche d'Or, the 'Golden Corniche'). On the approach to Agay, you get to enjoy many excellent views of craggy, burnished mountains tumbling down into open seas.

1 Agay

Agay is the only resort of any significant size on the Corniche, and a refreshing change from the pseudo-sophistication of some of its better-known sister resorts. Its attractive beach and small harbour lie snugly protected within a sheltered horseshoe-shaped bay.

From Agay you can take a detour inland, initially along the D100, and then turning right after a few kilometres along a twisting road through the hills for the superb viewpoints of the Pic du Cap Roux (452m/1,483ft), the Pic d'Aurelle (323m/1,060ft) and the Pic de l'Ours (496m/1,627ft).

The coast road from Agay leads to the smaller seaside centre of Anthéor and Anthéor-Plage (Beach). Le Trayas, just before Miramar, is the highest point on the Corniche. The road overlooks a rugged section of coastline, though there is an abrupt change of scene on the approach to Théoule-sur-Mer when Cannes and the densely developed Golfe de Napoule come into view.

2 La Napoule

The small resort of La Napoule, with its large, boat-filled harbour, marks the start of the Riviera proper. Its château, dating from the 14th century, was much altered by American sculptor Henry Clews at the start of the 20th century. Critics call it a tasteless folly. See if you agree by taking a guided tour (*tours available, Mar–Oct, Wed–Mon, afternoons; tel: 04 93 49 95 05*).
For the return leg of the tour, follow the N7 inland, a scenic road that skirts the northern slopes of the Massif de l'Esterel, following mainly the Roman route Via Aurelia. The Auberge des Adrets was the haunt of a highwayman in the 18th century. About 5km (3 miles) after the Auberge, turn left for Mont Vinaigre.

3 Mont Vinaigre

Mont Vinaigre, at 618m (2,028ft), is the highest point in the Massif (there are also spectacular views from the Col de l'Aire de l'Olivier just to the south). This is excellent walking country, with a good network of trails and picnic areas. *Return to the N7, a road that twists and turns on the descent to Fréjus.*

4 Chapelle Notre-Dame-de-Jérusalem

Stop off at this chapel. Its single chamber is brightly decorated with murals designed by Jean Cocteau. Further along the road, just a few kilometres from Fréjus is a Vietnamese pagoda, used as a Buddhist temple.

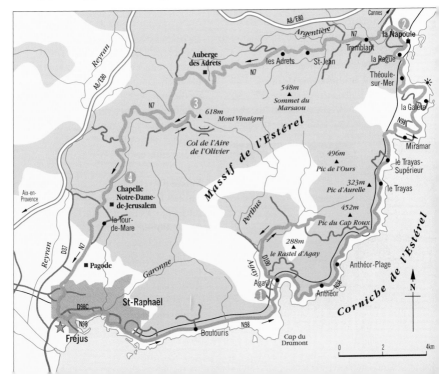

Alpes-Maritimes

The busiest stretch of the Côte d'Azur – including the tiny independent Principality of Monaco – lies between Cannes and the Italian border. This is the Riviera at its most incandescent and infuriating. The contrast between coast and country could not be more striking. Within an hour's drive of the Mediterranean is a *département* of hidden valleys, remote, inaccessible uplands and wild Alpine scenery.

From Picasso's prolific Antibes period

Antibes

The Cap d'Antibes promontory jutting out into the Mediterranean between Cannes and Nice is made up of two fashionable resorts, Antibes and Juan-les-Pins (*see pp100–101*). Antibes, on the eastern shore, is a honeypot for celebrities and the seriously rich. The millionaires in search of more privacy hide themselves away behind high fences in their exclusive mansions around Cap d'Antibes.

Antibes also attracts artists. Picasso's studio was at **Château Grimaldi**, an unmissable landmark on the headland

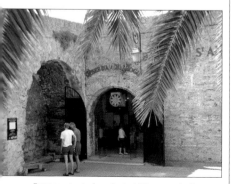

Entrance to Archaeological Museum, Antibes

above the old town. The medieval château and stout sea wall guard Antibes's characterful old quarter, far more enticing than the busy, bland modern town further inland. Look out among the narrow streets for the cathedral (noted for its magnificent early 18th-century doors) and unapologetically workaday covered market. The **Vieux Port** (Old Port) has been completely overshadowed by the massive modern harbour of neighbouring **Port Vauban** – mooring place of some of Europe's most fabulous yachts – overlooked by the 16th-century Fort Carré.

Musée d'Archéologie

Antibes has a long history. This museum tells the story of Etruscan, Greek, Roman and medieval settlement here.
Bastion St-André. Tel: 04 93 34 00 39. Open: Tue–Sun, 10am–noon & 2–6pm. Admission charge.

Musée Picasso

Picasso worked 'like a madman' for the

Alpes-Maritimes

six months, from July to December 1946, he spent at Château Grimaldi, achieving new heights of creative genius. His gift to Antibes for the use of the château was the artistic output of his stay. This outstanding collection forms the basis of the Picasso Museum, later enriched by his tapestries, ceramics, engravings and lithographs. It also has paintings and sculptures from other leading artists such as Miró, Modigliani, Léger and Ernst, and photographs of Picasso by Bill Brandt and Man Ray.

Château Grimaldi, place Marijol. Tel: 04 92 90 54 20. (Closed for renovation, due to reopen in Aug 2007.) Antibes is 11km (7 miles) northeast of Cannes.

Biot

The bond between Vallauris and Picasso (*see p118*) is mirrored by Biot's strong links with Fernand Léger (1881–1955). The inland village, north of Antibes, was Léger's home for the last few years of his life, and is the location of an important museum dedicated to the artist.

The medieval village, well known for its pottery and glassware (bubble glass is the local speciality), is a mixture of gateways, narrow lanes and sloping streets. Most visitors make for the rue St-Sébastien, where the potteries and glass shops are concentrated. You can see glassblowers at work in the Verrerie de Biot on chemin des Combes; the shop is on rue St-Sébastien.

Musée d'Histoire Locale

A restored kitchen is one of the exhibits in this museum of local life.

*Place de la Chapelle. Tel: 04 93 65 54 54.
Open: summer, Wed–Sun, 9am–noon
& 2–6pm; winter, Wed–Sun, 2–6pm.
Admission charge.*

Musée National Fernand Léger

A complete cross-section of the artist's work is on display, from early post-Cubism to the more direct man-and-industry canvases of his later period. *Off the D4 southeast of the village.
Tel: 04 92 91 50 30; www.musee-fernandleger.fr. Open: Wed–Mon,
10am–12.30pm & 2–6pm (till 5.30pm
Nov–Mar). Admission charge.*

Biot is on the D4, accessible off the N7, in the hills north of Antibes.

Cagnes-sur-Mer

The best part of ungainly, sprawling Cagnes-sur-Mer is Haut-de-Cagnes, the

The narrow streets of medieval Biot are full of craft studios and shops

These panels illustrate Biot's modern artistic legacy: the art of Fernand Léger

old medieval quarter set high on a ridge overlooking the coast. Here, you will find the usual 'perched village' picture of perfection: an ancient château (now a museum-cum-art gallery), exquisite homes and expensive restaurants, on a wooded outcrop prettified by sweet-scented ornamental gardens.

Back along the coast, Cagnes is famous for its racecourse-by-the-sea and associations with Auguste Renoir (1841–1919).

Musée Renoir

Parts of the house in which Renoir spent the last 11 years of his life look as if the artist is still at work.
La Maison de Renoir, Les Collettes.
Tel: 04 93 20 61 07.
Open: May–Sept, Wed–Mon,
10am–noon & 2–6pm; Oct–Apr,
Wed–Mon, 10am–noon & 2–5pm.
Admission charge.

Cagnes-sur-Mer is between Nice and Antibes.

Sophia-Antipolis

Driving between Nice and Cannes, you will see signs to Sophia-Antipolis, a vast science and technology park that forms part of Côte d'Azur's plans for continuing economic success. Although it has yet to eclipse tourism in its revenues, it has proved a fine base for investment in the 'sun belt'.

Set up as a long-term experiment in the early 1970s by P Lafitte, Sophia-Antipolis was conceived to be 'a city of science, culture and wisdom'. It took the Greek word for wisdom and paired it with the name for their ancient settlement at nearby Antibes. It is Europe's equivalent of California's Silicon Valley, and has, over the last three decades, morphed into a successful economic zone where the accent is now on R&D, telecommunications, IT, academia and other non-polluting industries. In total, some 1,100 companies have set up in Sophia-Antipolis employing over 21,000 staff. These include among the big names France Telecom, IBM, Siemens, AT&T and Alcatel.

In the dog-eat-dog IT business of the last few years, many of the companies that originally moved here have been absorbed by the others, but, significantly, few of the employees have considered relocating. Instead they have sought work within the Riviera area, or have set up their own firms.

Cannes

Cannes is big, busy and, amazingly enough, still beautiful in parts. In 1834 the English Lord Chancellor, Lord Brougham, arrived here after fleeing from cholera-stricken Nice. He liked what he saw, built a villa and – *voilà!* – the resort was born. Constant redevelopment continues apace on this febrile stretch of coast: the Cannes of today is not even a resort in the usual sense, more a year-round meeting place for businessmen, conference delegates and, of course, film stars.

Modern art in a Cannes street

The hub of modern Cannes is the **Palais des Festivals**, the vast convention centre overlooking the **Vieux Port** (Old Port). This great lump of a building, opened in 1982, illustrates where the priorities of the town planners lie. Everything is laid on with maximum convenience for the delegates. The immaculately tended main beaches are to the right and left, while the seafront boulevard de la Croisette is but a stone's throw away (the Carlton's sculpted, gleaming white façade really does look like a piece of wedding cake).

To return to reality, you have to climb the hill into **Le Suquet**, the old quarter on the western side of the port. Founded by the Romans, it later became the property of the monks of the **Îles de Lérins** a short distance offshore. Tour Le Suquet, the 11th-century watchtower crowning the summit, is a magnificent viewpoint. Also here is the Musée de la Castre and the Église Notre-Dame d'Espérance, completed in 1648.

If you are on a budget, then the restaurants in Le Suquet's narrow streets are your best bet for eating out. Back in the main town, rue d'Antibes and rue Meynadier are Cannes's fashionable shopping thoroughfares, though for more down-to-earth produce there is the covered market, the Marché Forville.

The quietest side of Cannes is at La Croisette at the far end of the seafront boulevard. But if you really want to get away from it all, then take the 15-minute boat trip from the Vieux Port to the tranquil islands known collectively as the Îles de Lérins: **St-Honorat**, with its monastic associations, and the larger **Ste-Marguerite**.

Mougins, a short distance inland from Cannes, is a delightful perched village of expensive restaurants and exclusive shops. It stands on a 260-m (853-ft) high outcrop, insulated from the busy world at its feet.

Musée de la Castre

Located in the old citadel, the museum contains antiquities from many countries and cultures – Mediterranean, Egyptian, Far Eastern, South American, etc. There is also a permanent exhibition of Provençal landscapes.

Place de la Castre, Le Suquet. Tel: 04 93 38 55 26. Open: Oct–Mar, Tue–Sun, 10am–1pm & 2–5pm; Sept & Apr–May 10am–1pm & 2–6pm; July–Aug, Tue–Sun, 10am–1pm & 3–7pm. Admission charge.

Musée de la Mer (Museum of the Sea)

This museum is within the fort on the island of Ste-Marguerite. Not just maritime in theme, its exhibits include items from local shipwrecks, artefacts excavated on the island, and the rooms of the old state prison at the fort, including the cell of the fabled Man in the Iron Mask.

Fort Royal, Île Ste-Marguerite. Tel: 04 93 38 55 26. Open: summer, Wed–Mon, 10.30am–1.15pm & 2.15– 5.45pm; winter, Wed–Mon, 10.30am–1.15pm & 2.15–4.45pm. Admission charge.

The old seaside resort of Cannes caters to an increasing number of visitors

Cannes Film Festival

There is only one place for the world's film-makers to be in May – Cannes, home of the International Film Festival. For two weeks the resort swarms with producers, directors, stars, starlets, minders, has-beens, hangers-on, deal-makers, journalists, moguls and would-be moguls. Deals are struck by hotel pools or in expensive restaurants in an atmosphere as unreal as anything created on a Hollywood set.

Born of rivalry

Curiously, all this hype and hysteria would never have come about at all had it not been for Benito Mussolini. The Italian dictator inaugurated the Venice Film Festival in the mid-1930s. The French, in retaliation for the fact that all the major prizes went to Fascist-oriented films, devised a rival festival. Their timing was less than serendipitous: set for a launch in September 1939, the festival was postponed until 1947 owing to the outbreak of war.

The new festival was not an overnight success. In the mid-50s, Brigitte Bardot made a huge impact at Cannes, and by the end of the decade American influence – and money – transformed the festival into a frenetic event characterised by wheeling and dealing, unbridled excess and controlled chaos.

Coming of age

Cannes in the 1960s became Hollywood's shop window in Europe, and as the TV industry expanded worldwide, followed by video, satellite and cable, the scale of the festival increased dramatically. Today, about 50,000 people descend on Cannes each year. The best film is awarded the Palme d'Or, the highest accolade in the film world after the almighty Oscar.

Following the impact Brigitte Bardot made here in the mid-50s, the festival at Cannes has become the most glamorous event on the international film circuit.

Facing page: A glorious setting for the Film Festival

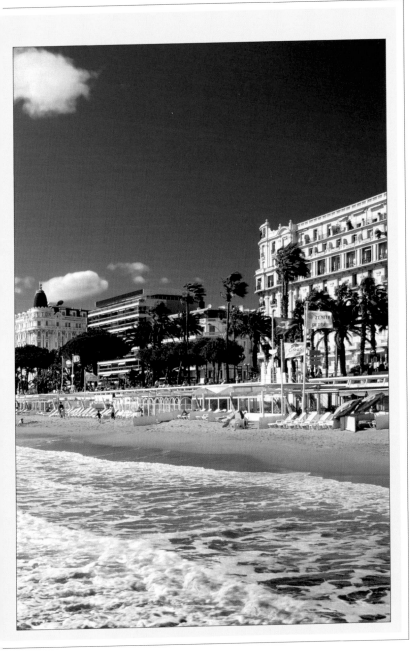

Eze

Of all the perched villages inland from the coast, Eze is the most dramatic. It is not so much perched as precariously balanced on a jagged, precipitous outcrop. The easiest approach is along the N7 – you can, if you are lucky, find a space in the car park at the foot of the village and then walk up into the maze of narrow vaulted passageways, crooked steps and secretive corners. Inevitably, it is nowadays almost entirely a tourist village of galleries, restaurants and shops, yet they fail to eclipse Eze's breathtaking setting 470m (1,542ft) above sea level, and the integrity of its restored medieval architecture.

Paradoxically, its strongest point – the original castle – has suffered most from the ravages of time. The 14th-century Chapelle des Pénitents Blancs on place du Planet is in rather better condition. Its chief glory is an unusual Catalan crucifix of the mid-13th century which depicts a smiling Christ.

Jardin Exotique

This unusual garden of cacti and succulents is located amongst the ruins of Eze's castle.
Tel: 04 93 41 26 00. Open: summer. daily, 9am–8pm; winter, daily, 9am–dusk. Admission charge.

Eze is between Monaco and Nice.

Gourdon

Spectacularly located, Gourdon is another sheer-sided perched village. Although there are one or two classy shops selling perfume and soap, it is best to ignore the tacky tourist knick-knacks and concentrate instead on the castle with superb Le Nôtre-designed gardens and magnificent view of the coast.

Château de Gourdon

The immaculately restored 13th-century castle has an excellent display of arms and armour, and an interesting art collection.
Tel: 04 93 09 68 02. Open: June–Sept, daily, 11am–1pm & 2–7pm; Oct–May, Wed–Mon, 2–6pm. Admission charge.

Gourdon is on the D3, 14km (9 miles) northeast of Grasse.

The panorama from Eze's Jardin Exotique, at the summit of this precipitous village

Fountain and flowers adorn sweet-smelling Grasse's place aux Aires

Grasse

This charming town, set in shallow but sheltering hill country less than 20km (12 miles) from the coast, has a graceful, calming air. Its surrounding meadowlands yield the fragrant flowers that have made Grasse famous as a perfume town. Whenever you visit you will be assailed by fragrance: mimosas in spring, roses and lavender in summer, jasmine in autumn. The town has not been able to distance itself completely from the overdevelopment along the coast. But although Grasse has its modern housing and high-technology parks, it is still an appealing mixture of the handsome and the humble: fine old buildings and traditional workaday shopping streets.

These two contrasting sides to Grasse are closest together along the elegant terraced gardens in front of the grand Palais des Congrès. Take the steps down into rue Jean-Ossola and you are immediately enclosed within an old town of narrow streets. A daily market is held at place aux Aires, while place du Petit-Puy is the site of Grasse's cathedral, dating from the 12th century. It is well worth devoting some time to this part of Grasse and its museums, despite the town's overwhelming

association with perfume (*see p100*). There are some 30 *parfumeries* in and around the town (ask for details at the Office de Tourisme, Palais des Congrès – *tel: 04 93 36 66 66*).

Musée International de la Parfumerie

The museum deals with the history and manufacture of perfume.
8 place du Cours. Tel: 04 97 05 58 00. Open: June–Sept, daily, 10am–12.30pm & 1.30–6.30pm; Oct–May, Wed–Sun, 10am–12.30pm & 2–5.30pm (closed for renovation until Sept 2006). Admission charge.

Villa-Musée Fragonard

Works by Fragonard can be seen in this 18th-century villa in which the artist lived. The Parfumerie Fragonard, at 20 boulevard Fragonard, is a museum of perfume (admission free).
23 boulevard Fragonard.
Tel: 04 97 05 58 00. Open: June–Sept, daily, 10am–12.30pm & 1.30–6.30pm; Oct–May, Wed–Sun, 10am–12.30pm & 2–5.30pm. Admission charge.
Grasse is 20km (12 miles) northwest of Cannes.

Not just a pretty face, she tells you the time (but only up to 3 o'clock): sundial in Gourdon

Isola 2000

This is one for the skiing enthusiasts. Despite the fact that it is one of the southernmost Alpine resorts and only 1½ hours from Nice, Isola has a good snow record. If you are familiar with other French Alpine resorts, then Isola will hold no surprises. The functional approach, devoid of any Alpine charm, does at least deliver super-convenient doorstep skiing. Its unimaginative name derives from its altitude.

The resort, accessible by the tortuous D2205 through the Gorges of the Tinée, is only a few kilometres from the Italian border. Its proximity to the Parc National du Mercantour (*see pp137–8*) gives some credence to its claim of being a year-round resort, especially since accommodation costs are much lower in the summer 'off season'.

Further along the Tinée Valley is **Auron**, the oldest ski resort in the Alpes-Maritimes.

Juan-les-Pins

Juan-les-Pins is the place to be seen at night on the exclusive peninsula of Cap d'Antibes (*see also p90*). By day, you wonder what all the fuss is about, for Juan-les-Pins is an unexceptional little resort, neat and tidy but disappointingly bland. It wakes up after the sun goes down, when the clubs, bars

The heady scents of Provence bottled for your pleasure

and restaurants attract the Cap's well-heeled villa owners and glamour-seekers. F Scott Fitzgerald, aided and abetted by a few rich fellow Americans, colonised this stretch of coast in the 1920s, creating the fabulous myth that Juan-les-Pins has been living off ever since. Part of Fitzgerald's novel *Tender Is the Night* is set here, and he wrote to a friend, 'I'd like to live and die on the French Riviera.'

Musée Naval et Napoléonien
Model ships, along with items relating to Napoleon's return from exile on Elba and other memorabilia.
Batterie du Grillon, boulevard John-F-Kennedy (at Cap d'Antibes south of Juan-les-Pins). Tel: 04 93 61 45 32.
Open: winter, Tue–Sat, 10am–4.30pm;

Picture-perfect expanses of sun 'n' sand

summer, Tue–Sat 10am–6pm. Closed: Oct. Admission charge.

Juan-les-Pins is a few kilometres from Antibes, on the opposite side of the Cap d'Antibes peninsula.

Beach addicts enjoy Juan-les-Pins by day, but after sundown the place really comes alive

Menton

'Ma ville est un jardin' ('My town is a garden') claims the tourist literature for Menton – and for once it is right. Menton, almost within shouting distance of the Italian border, is the French Riviera's floral town *par excellence*. Its exceptional sunshine record, coupled with a subtropical climate and a patently garden-mad town council, have conspired to produce a resort bursting with colourful floral beds, luscious orange, lemon and palm trees, and beautiful award-winning areas of greenery. Where else would you find a place that holds a Fête du Citron in February, a festival of floats and tableaux made entirely of flowers, oranges and, of course, lemons?

Prettily packaged local herbs make good gifts

Menton, unlike its more illustrious neighbours, has not embraced the growth-at-any-cost philosophy. Consequently, it is still a true resort as opposed to a conurbation by the sea. The **Vieille Ville** (Old Town), a cluster of pastel-shaded houses riddled with steep alleyways, has an almost Italianate air. All passageways eventually lead to place de la Conception on the highest ground above the **Vieux Port** (Old Port) and two ornate religious sites – the **Église de la Conception** and the **Église St-Michel**.

The sturdy fortified building on quai Napoléon pays homage to Jean Cocteau, though fans of the artist will also want to see the way he transformed the humble Salle des Mariages (registry office) in the Hôtel de Ville (Town Hall) in 1957.

West of quai Napoléon along baie du Soleil lies Menton's main beach. The promenade – and, for that matter, the entire resort – has an unexpectedly genteel, relaxed air, due in no small part

to its popularity with elderly retired folk attracted by Menton's calm, sunny climate. The lucky ones are able to afford the villas in the hilly **Garavan** district east of the Vieux Port, a gorgeous garden suburb thick with exotic vegetation and blessed with marvellous sea views. Avenue Katherine-Mansfield, named after the writer who had a retreat here, winds its way through this privileged quarter. Here you will also find the **Jardin des Colombières**, the best in the Garavan district and one of the finest on the Riviera.

Jardin du Val Rahmeh
Many species of both tropical and subtropical plants thrive in this botanical garden of the National Museum of Natural History.
Tel: 04 93 35 86 72. Open: Apr–Sept, daily, 10am–12.30pm & 3.30–6.30pm; Oct–Mar, daily, 10am–12.30pm & 2–5pm. Admission charge.

Musée Jean-Cocteau
Cocteau's paintings are beautifully presented in this 17th-century bastion. The painter and poet, who lived locally, designed the mosaic floor and donated many works of art.
Bastion du Vieux Port, quai Napoléon III. Tel: 04 93 57 72 30. Open: Wed–Mon, 10am–noon & 2–6pm. Admission charge. To see more of Cocteau's work visit the Chapelle Nôtre-Dame-de-Jérusalem near Fréjus (see p89).

Musée de la Préhistoire Régionale
The star attraction at this museum is the famous 'Menton Man', a 30,000-year-old skull. Local traditions and culture are also covered.
Rue Lorédan-Larchey. Tel: 04 93 35 84 64. Open: as for Musée Jean-Cocteau. Free admission.

Place de la Conception
The dominant building here is the baroque Église St-Michel, pink and ochre outside and ornate within.

The sunken square just outside is the venue for an atmospheric summer festival of chamber music. Close by is the Église de la Conception, built for the White Penitents in 1685. Restored in the 1980s, it has a wonderfully exuberant – or over-the-top, depending on taste – baroque interior. (A third religious site, for the Black Penitents – the **Chapelle des Pénitents-Noirs** – stands a short distance away at the bottom of rue de Bréa.) The best way to see the square is at night, during the famous summer chamber music festival.

Salle des Mariages
Cocteau's swirling, extravagant murals succeed admirably in his aim to 'create a theatrical setting . . . to offset the officialdom of a civil ceremony'.
Hôtel de Ville, place Ardoiono, rue de la République. Tel: 04 92 10 50 00. Open: Mon–Fri, 8.30am–12.30pm & 2–5pm. Admission charge.

Popular since the 19th century, picturesque Menton climbs up from its harbour

The literary tradition in Provence reaches all the way back to the troubadours, whose poems of courtly love encapsulate the most romantic aspect of medievalism. They were written in the Provençal language, which enjoyed a revival in the 19th century under the influence of poet Frédéric Mistral, who was awarded the Nobel Prize for Literature in 1904.

Marcel Pagnol (1895–1974) from Aubagne was a writer of novels, poems and short stories. His vision of Provence was captured in the atmospheric stories that became the award-winning films *Jean de Florette* and *Manon des sources*. Jean Giono (1895–1970) was similarly

inspired by the landscapes and the people of Provence – in his case, the area around his birthplace, Manosque.

The perfect workplace

Provence has arguably cast an even deeper spell over outsiders beguiled by its promise of sunshine and sensuality. In comparison to the bucolic works of its resident writers, literature of another kind was being written on the Riviera by leading American writers like F Scott Fitzgerald and Ernest Hemingway after World War I. In an era of prohibition and puritanism, they fled from what they regarded as the cultural wasteland of America to enjoy an easier lifestyle in the sun. Fitzgerald gave an evocative portrait of life in Cap d'Antibes in the 1920s in *Tender Is the Night*, but the idyll was bruised by his wife Zelda's affair with a young French aviator.

A writers' colony

Hemingway and his wife Hadley lived in a threesome on the Riviera with the American heiress Pauline Pfeiffer before moving on. In 1930 Aldous Huxley joined a writers' colony in the South of France, his neighbours including Thomas Mann and Cyril Connolly. The English novelist Somerset Maugham bought a house in Cap

Ferrat in 1926 and spent at least six months every year there until his death in 1965, entertaining such celebrities as the Aga Khan, Winston Churchill, Noël Coward and Jean Cocteau.

Facing page above: scene from *Manon des Sources*; below: a sign commemorates a local hero
This page: one of many foreign residents in the region – Aldous Huxley

An earlier arrival on the Riviera was the New Zealand-born British writer Katherine Mansfield, who died tragically young from TB. On a happier note, the 18-year-old Françoise Sagan achieved fame in the 1950s with her novel *Bonjour Tristesse*, a sharply defined love story set in a villa near Cannes. Other writers closely linked with the Riviera include Graham Greene and Anthony Burgess.

Monaco

Even for those used to the tightly packed, over-hyped Riviera, Monaco comes as something of a shock to the system. Not one square millimetre of Monaco is wasted. High-rise buildings are stacked up within touching distance of each other, making the most of the limited space available in this 3-km (2-mile) long tax haven. Historically a Greek, then a Roman colony, Monaco was bought from the Genoese by the Grimaldis. In 1346 the Grimaldi Charles 1 started building a fortress on the rocks of Monaco. Despite battles with the French crown resulting in the reduction of the principality, the Grimaldi dynasty has ruled over what has proved to be the world's longest-lasting democracy headed by a monarch.

All the best boats moor in the high-society harbour in Monaco

Today money is Monaco's *raison d'être*. The opulent main casino is the most overt manifestation of the serious wealth that underpins this home of millionaires who, perfectly legally, avoid paying any income tax. And all this wealth is protected in more ways than one. Monaco has more policemen per square kilometre than any other place in the world.

Changing the guard

You might think that Monaco's artificiality, over-indulgence and self-satisfaction make for a pretty rich diet – and you would be correct. But you should at least sample a little of it. There are compensations: the principality's immaculate, litter-free streets, its beautifully manicured gardens, and the undeniable spectacle of one of the world's most glamorous harbours full of some of the world's most expensive ocean-going palaces.

The densely populated principality is divided into a number of districts. Most visitor interest is concentrated in **Monaco-Ville**, the promontory west of the harbour (which contains the majority of the historic sites) and glitzy Monte Carlo (the casino, conference and hotel district) to the east.

Jardin Animalier
Tropical flora and fauna flourish in these gardens.
Terrasses de Fontvieille. Tel: (377) 93 25 18 31. Open: June–Sept, daily, 9am–noon & 2–7pm; Mar–May, daily, 10am–noon & 2–6pm; Oct–Feb, daily, 10am–noon & 2–5pm. Admission charge.

Jardin Exotique
Thousands of different exotic plants – including giant cacti – grow amongst rocks in this beautiful garden. You can also visit a cave with spectacular stalagmite and stalactite formations, and a museum of prehistory.
Boulevard du Jardin Exotique. Tel: (377) 93 15 29 80. Open: May–Sept, daily, 9am–7pm; rest of the year 9am–dusk. Admission charge.

Musée Historial des Princes de Monaco (Wax Museum)
Episodes from the history of the Grimaldis are depicted here.
27 rue Basse. Tel: (377) 93 30 39 05. Open: mid-May–mid-Sept, daily, 9am–7pm; mid-Sept–mid-May, daily, 9am–sunset. Admission charge.

Musée Océanographique
Housed in a stunning neoclassical building poised over the cliff face, this museum of marine sciences contains the usual maritime specimens plus a famous 90-tank aquarium.
Avenue Saint-Martin. Tel: (377) 93 15 36 00; www.oceano.mc. Open: June–Aug, daily, 9am–8pm; Apr, May & Sept, daily, 9am–7pm; Oct–Mar, daily, 10am–6pm. Admission charge.

Palais Princier (Prince's Palace)
Outstanding features include the Italian-style gallery, the blue-and-gold Louis XV Salon and the Throne Room. The palace's South Wing contains a museum of Napoleonic souvenirs and historic archives.
Place du Palais. Tel: (377) 93 25 18 31. Open: June–Sept, daily, 9.30am–6pm; Oct, daily, 10am–5pm. Closed: Nov–May. Call for museum opening times. Admission charge.

Vieux Monaco
This historic part of Monaco has a number of interesting buildings in its narrow streets and alleys. Among these are the Palais de Justice, the fountain in place St-Nicolas, the placette Bosio, the Chapelle de la Paix, and the long brick Rampe Major linking La Condamine and the place du Palais.

The royal palace of Monaco

Walk: Monaco

This walk concentrates on Monaco-Ville, the rocky promontory above the harbour dominated by the Palais Princier (Prince's Palace). In comparison to the hustle and bustle of the port below and the shops and casinos of Monte Carlo to the east, this part of the principality – the picturesque Old Town, a mixture of narrow streets, open spaces and gardens – seems positively sedate.

The walk can be comfortably completed in half a day.

From La Racasse hairpin (a name familiar to fans of Formula One Grand Prix racing) in La Condamine harbour and business district, walk along quai Antoine 1er, taking a short detour left along the sea wall to the mouth of the port. Return to the yacht club on the quay, then climb the steps up towards the

Monaco's cathedral contains the tomb of the much-loved Princess Grace

tubby-looking Fort Antoine, continuing the climb into the gardens (signposted Palais, Musée).

1 Quay walk and gardens

The quay walk and gardens give you some idea of what Monaco must have been like before the developers took over. The quieter side of the harbour leads to restful, shady gardens rising above Fort Antoine, an 18th-century defensive fortification now used as an outdoor theatre (*tel: (377) 93 15 80 00*). *Walk through the gardens to the Musée Océanographique, then take the pedestrianised street opposite – ruelle des Écoles – for place de la Visitation, turning left here for rue Princesse Marie de Lorraine.*

2 Rue Princesse Marie de Lorraine

This cobbled street leads to the heart of the Old Town. The **Chapelle de la Miséricorde**, built 1639–45, was the seat of the Brotherhood of the Black Penitents, and contains a remarkable figure of Christ carved in wood. *Continue down rue Basse, a very narrow* *street lined with shops and cafés, to the Musée Historial des Princes de Monaco (Wax Museum). From here, the street becomes even narrower before opening out into the huge open square, place du Palais.*

3 Place du Palais

Place du Palais fronts the Palais Princier, the home of the Monégasque royal family, a mainly 19th-century building castellated for decorative effect only. The Changing of the Guard takes place here at 11.55am every day, a ceremony performed in full dress uniform (white in summer, black in winter). The lofty place du Palais is a natural vantage point. Lined with cannons cast in the reign of Louis XIV, it looks down directly into the harbour, across to high-rise Monte Carlo and along the coast as far east as the Cape of Bordighera in Italy.

Leave place du Palais by rue Colonel Bellando de Castro, which brings you to the Palais de Justice and cathedral.

4 Cathédrale

The 19th-century cathedral, built in Romanesque-Byzantine style on the site of a 13th-century church dedicated to St Nicholas, contains tombs of former princes of Monaco. An episcopal throne in white marble and early 16th-century reredos are amongst its noteworthy features, though the cathedral's most-visited shrine is the tomb of Princess Grace (*open: daily, 8.30am–7pm, until 6pm in winter*).

Return to place du Palais and descend this rocky outcrop by La Rampe Major, a staircase in the side of the cliff. Cross avenue de la Porte Neuve and follow avenue du Port back to the harbourside.

M o n a c o

This street in busy Nice, with its stuccoed buildings, has a distinctly Italianate air

Nice

This noisy, seductive, teeming, vibrant city-by-the-sea takes some getting used to. You do not come to Nice for a quiet time; neither do you come for a standard seaside holiday. You come because of Nice's exhaustive stock of first-class museums; you come to sample its bubbling nightlife; you come to take a stroll down the famous promenade des Anglais; you come for business, not pleasure, for Nice is the nucleus of a dynamic southern economy dubbed the 'California of Europe'. You might – if you have the time – even spend an hour or so on the beach.

Nice is France's fifth-largest city – though it appears larger than it is as it cloaks its wooded hills, spreads behind into the fertile coastal plain and inches its way north and south along the shoreline. It enjoys a fine climate as it is largely protected from the bone-chilling *mistral* but is cooled by breezes from the deep blue Mediterranean Baie des Anges (Bay of Angels) during summer. A port, a resort and an ever-growing city, it has vastly improved its face in the last decade and is once again enjoying popularity with visitors. It is a wonderful city to discover and an excellent base from which to explore the allure of the Côte d'Azur and its magnificent hinterland.

It was the Romans who founded Cemenelum (now the Cimiez district) but the English, French and Italians have all had a hand in creating the Nice of today. English aristocrats gave the benevolent climate their stamp of approval. Italian nobility ruled here until 1860, when they handed the city over to the French and Nizza became Nice. This mixed bag of influences is most apparent in the central area, where you will find the convincingly Italianate place Masséna (which really should be across the border!), the medieval **Vieille Ville**, the *belle époque* architecture, the extravagantly spacious gardens, the animated daily market along cours Saleya, and the main shopping streets. The one viewpoint from which it all starts to make sense is the 92-m (302-ft) high **Le Château**, not a castle but a wooded park. Beyond the shoreline, and up in the hills, are a number of lavish villas such as those in the Mont-Boron and Cimiez district – many still privately owned – that were constructed during the *belle époque* and fashionable Fifties. For the visitor with time, they are also worth looking at.

The only way to begin to get to know Nice is on foot. Many places of interest are within reasonable walking distance of the strip of coast that runs for a kilometre or so from Le Château hill along the promenade des Anglais. For the less energetic, a *petit train* (tourist train departing daily from the tourist office by the Jardins Albert 1er) plies the most popular tourist routes and helps you get your bearings – you can always go back by foot later.

Note that admission is free to museums on the first and third Sunday of the month and that a museum card (moderate fee) offers free access for a week to practically all of Nice's museums.

Other places to visit include the Villa Arson (contemporary modern art exhibits), Musée Terra Amata (a prehistoric collection and reconstruction of a 400,000-year-old campsite), the baroque Cathédrale de Ste-Réparate and its square, Jardin Botanique (a fine collection of plants and trees, located in the western part of Nice), Palais de Justice, Opéra and the

vibrant morning market in cours Saleya. Further afield, the exclusive Saint-Jean-Cap-Ferrat and Villefranche are definitely worth visiting for their views, fine ports and numerous wealthy homes (some still inhabited by royalty), all discreetly veiled by lush palms and imposing walls.

Cathédrale Orthodoxe Russe de Saint Nicolas

An anomaly – but a glitteringly beautiful one – on the Nice horizon built in 1912 by the Tsarina Maria Feodorovna in memory of her son, the Grand Duke Nicholas. It was the first, and remains the finest, Russian church outside Russia.
Avenue Nicholas II. Tel: 04 93 96 88 02. Open: summer, daily, 9am–noon & 2.30–5pm; rest of the year, daily, 9.15am–noon & 2.30–5.30pm. Admission charge.

Exhibit in the Museum of Modern Art, just one of Nice's many fine museums

Hôtel Negresco

Nice's most famous landmark, this exotic *belle époque* hotel was built for the Romanian Henri Negresco in 1912 by Belgian architect Edouard Niermans. It has hosted amongst others Queen Elizabeth II, Emperor Hirohito, Churchill, Rockefeller, the Beatles, Picasso, Charlie Chaplin, Cary Grant, Marlon Brando, Andrew Lloyd Webber and Frank Sinatra. Still the city's most exclusive hotel, it enjoys immense popularity for its historic past, contemporary luxury and prime position on the promenade.
37 promenade des Anglais.
Tel: 04 93 16 64 00.

Musée d'Archéologie

Exhibits span the Bronze Age down to the Middle Ages. It stands on the edge of excavated 3rd-century Roman baths with 5th-century religious buildings and offers a number of archaeological items found on this Roman site. Take time afterwards to explore the garden of the amphitheatre of Cimiez. This is the site of Nice's annual Jazz Festival.
160 avenue des Arènes de Cimiez.
Tel: 04 93 81 59 57. Open: Wed–Mon, 10am–6pm. Admission charge.

Musée des Arts Asiatiques

Gleaming white marble in this Kenzo Tange-designed museum provides the backdrop for this collection of classical and contemporary works from different regions of Asia. The museum is located on an island in an artificial lake in the midst of a 7-hectare (17-acre) garden.
405 promenade des Anglais. Tel 04 92 29 37 00; www.arts-asiatiques.com. Open:
summer, Wed–Mon, 10am–6pm; winter, Wed–Mon, 10am–5pm. Free admission.

Musée d'Art Moderne et d'Art Contemporain

A permanent collection consisting mainly of neo-Realism and Pop Art – definitely for aficionados of modern art. There is a great view of Old Nice from the rooftop.
Promenade des Arts. Tel: 04 93 62 61 62. Open: Wed–Mon, 10am–6pm. Admission charge.

Musée des Beaux-Arts (Museum of Fine Arts)

The gallery has a large collection of 17th- to 19th-century paintings plus sculptures, and also hosts temporary art exhibits. Once the private home of Ukrainian Princess Kotschoubey, the elegant mansion also has pleasant shady gardens.
33 avenue des Baumettes. Tel: 04 92 15 28 28. Open: Tue–Sun 10am–6pm. Admission charge.

Musée d'Histoire Naturelle

Over a million objects fill this large museum, which is a treasure trove for the young.
60 bis boulevard Risso. Tel: 04 97 13 46 80. Open: Tue–Sun, 10am–6pm. Free admission.

Musée Franciscan et Monastère de Cimez

Devoted to the life and work of the Franciscan monks, the museum includes three Gothic paintings by renowned local artist Louis Bréa. The beautiful flower-filled gardens are also open to the public.

Place du Monastére. Tel: 04 93 81 00 04.
Open: Mon–Sat, 10am–noon & 3–6pm.
Free admission.

Musée International d'Art Naïf Anatoly Jakovsky

A fine collection of naïve art from the last two centuries acquired from all over the world. Located in the former home of the perfumier François Coty.
Chateau Sainte-Helene, avenue Val-Marie. Tel: 04 93 71 78 33. Open: Wed–Mon, 10am–6pm. Admission charge.

Musée Matisse

Matisse settled in Nice in 1917 and died here in 1954. His personal collection is displayed in a splendid 17th-century villa in Cimiez, Nice's smart suburb.
164 avenue des Arènes de Cimiez. Tel: 04 93 81 08 08; www.musee-matisse-nice.org. Open: Wed–Mon, 10am–6pm. Admission charge.

Musée National Marc Chagall

This is the place for lovers of the colourful work of Russian émigré, Chagall. His fabulist style is given full expression in a series of paintings, a 'Biblical Message' based on the Old Testament. But many of his other works – paintings, stained glass, gouaches, drawings and mosaics – are also well displayed in this important museum.
Avenue du Docteur-Ménard. Tel: 04 93 53 87 20. Open: summer, Wed–Mon, 10am–6pm; winter, Wed–Mon, 10am–5pm. Admission charge.

Palais Lascaris

Decorative arts dating from the baroque and fabulous state rooms

Museum of Fine Arts, Nice

decorated with 17th- and 18th-century frescoes make this one of the more impressive places to visit. The palace is noted for its magnificent baroque staircase.
15 rue Droite. Tel: 04 93 62 05 54. Open: Wed–Mon, 10am–6pm. Free admission.

St-Paul-de-Vence

Some perched villages are famous for their restaurants, others for their real estate. St-Paul is famous for its art. Galleries are everywhere, though the usual crafts and clothes shops are not exactly thin on the ground. The village has made a lot of concessions to tourists: few of the medieval houses along its main street seem to serve their original purpose, having been converted into expensive galleries and bright T-shirt and fast-food joints. Its arty associations reach their zenith at the Fondation Maeght. The village even displays its cultural pretensions on its pavements, which are decorated with pebbles arranged in artistic swirls and patterns. Nevertheless, St-Paul has a distinctive charm.

The main gate into the village is alongside the Café de la Place, a lovely old-fashioned café complete with *boules* pitch outside. St-Paul's unbroken ring of 16th-century walls protects a medieval village dominated by a hilltop church. The 12th-century Église de St-Paul-de-Vence has a tall 18th-century bell tower that is almost matched in height by the giant palm tree growing beside it.

Fondation Maeght

Created in the 1950s by collectors Aimé and Marguerite Maeght, this unique purpose-built arts centre eschews the established concepts of entrance, exit and the *sense de la visite*. Nothing is arranged conventionally. Outside, you will encounter modern sculpture set tongue-in-cheek against water, trees and stone walls. Permanent and temporary exhibitions are held in the centre's airy split-level galleries.
Route Passe-Prest. Tel: 04 93 32 81 63; www.fondation-maeght.com.
Open: July–Sept, daily, 10am–7pm; Oct–June, daily, 10am–12.30pm & 2.30–6pm. Admission charge.

Musée d'Histoire Locale

The most important events in the lives of the people of St-Paul are reflected in the museum's tableaux and exhibits.
Place de la Castre. Tel: 04 93 32 41 13. Open: Mon & Wed–Sat, 10am–noon & 2–5pm. Closed: Nov. Admission charge.

St-Paul-de-Vence is in the hills between Nice and Antibes.

Saorge

High in the Alpes-Maritimes close to the Italian border, this village is accessible by the N204 through the Gorges de Saorge, a dramatic defile carved by the tumbling River Roya. The fortified village was built to control communications into the high country of the Haute Roya, a hybrid area of Italian and French influences which only became French territory in 1947.

Saorge, its terraces piled haphazardly one above the other on a savage slope, is a spectacular sight. This *village empilé* (stacked village) is the mountain equivalent of the perched villages along the coast. Its impossibly steep cobbled alleyways and confusing tiers of streets eventually lead up to the 15th-century Église St-Sauveur and a Franciscan monastery. Further up still is the isolated 11th-century Romanesque chapel of Madone del Poggio.

Higher up the valley, close to the

border, is the unequivocally Italianate village of **Tende**, while to the south lies restful **Breil-sur-Roya**, centre of the local olive oil industry (*see pp160–61*). *Saorge is close to the Italian border, 47km (29 miles) north of Menton.*

Tourrettes-sur-Loup

This picturesque village is partly misnamed. Its medieval towers (*tours*) are evident enough, but the River Loup is elsewhere, in the rolling, wooded hills to the south. The village's Grand-Rue is also misleadingly named: narrow, crooked and atmospheric, it winds its way past ancient, rough-stoned houses, some of which have been converted into potteries, craft workshops and galleries, while others still await restoration.

From Tourrettes, take the D2210 to Pont-du-Loup, turning northwards along the D6 for the craggy **Gorges du Loup**. The narrow road, chiselled out of the rock face, wriggles up a steep-sided valley beside the foaming river. At the top end of the gorge, return south on the D3, which climbs to give wonderful views down into the vertical-sided valley. *Tourrettes-sur-Loup is about 22km (14 miles) northeast of Grasse.*

Saorge, a 'stacked village' dramatically perched on the mountain side

The vivid colours and intense light of the South of France have enticed many artists to Provence, including Van Gogh (see pp56–7), Monet and Renoir in the 19th century, and Matisse and Picasso in the 20th.

19th century

Claude Monet first visited the region in 1883 and returned in 1888 to stay in Antibes and Juan-les-Pins. He followed the custom of the age by spending winter and early spring in the south and shrewdly painted local beauty spots to attract collectors.

Auguste Renoir spent the winter of 1889–90 in the south and settled in Cagnes-sur-Mer in 1905. Crippled by rheumatoid arthritis, he continued to paint with a brush wedged between his rigid fingers, completing more than 6,000 pictures in his lifetime.

Paul Cézanne was a home-grown talent. He spent much of his life in his birthplace, Aix-en-Provence (where he died in 1906), gradually establishing a reputation which today places him as a master of Post-Impressionism and one of the forerunners of modern art.

20th century

Henri Matisse and Raoul Dufy were among the *fauves* ('wild beasts'), so called because of their aggressive use of strong colour, who also followed the Impressionists. The most influential artist of the 20th century, Pablo Picasso, often spent his summers at Juan-les-Pins between the wars, and in 1946 he left Paris for good to settle in the Riviera. The lifestyle had a liberating effect, and even in extreme old age he created 1,000 works of art in five years. A lifetime of creativity ended in April 1973, when he died at the age of 92.

The success of Picasso and Matisse offended another great artist associated with the Riviera, Marc Chagall. He

MARC CHAGALL
LES ANNÉES MÉDITERRANÉENNES, 1949-1985
3 JUILLET - 31 OCTOBRE 1994

ŒUVRES PROFANES   V   ŒUVRES BIBLIQUES

settled there to show the world he was their equal, moving to St-Jean-Cap-Ferrat in 1949. In the 1950s Nice produced the school of artists known as

Chagall made the Riviera his permanent home, but Picasso (above) also spent many summers painting there

Nouveaux Realistes, who reacted against the Abstract Expressionism popular in America and the lyrical Abstraction of Paris. One of its exponents, Yves Klein, coated the bodies of nude models with paint and ordered them to crawl over the canvases. Whatever would Van Gogh have made of that?

Vallauris

If you do not like pottery, then give
Vallauris a miss. The town's love affair
with pots is flaunted quite
unselfconsciously. Oversized urns,
serving as giant flowerpots, line the smart
shopping streets in the modern town
beneath the old quarter of the Vieille
Ville with its Renaissance château.

Vallauris's pottery pedigree dates back
to Roman times. By the end of World
War II, the industry was on its last legs.
Revival came when Pablo Picasso took
an interest, spending two prolific years
at the Madoura pottery workshop in the
town. Other artists, including Chagall,
followed in his wake. Vallauris was back
in the pottery business.

Most of the potteries – of varying
quality and value – are located along the
main street, avenue Georges-
Clemenceau; the Madoura pottery,
which still sells Picasso designs, is off the
main street along avenue des Anciens
Combattants d'AFN. In the place de la
Libération, the town's main square and
marketplace, is the life-size bronze
statue *Man Holding a Sheep*, Picasso's
gift to the town in 1950.

Vallauris is famous for its pottery

Colourful church façade in Vence

Musée Municipal

Housed in the château, the museum
contains an excellent collection of
ceramics – including pieces by Picasso –
and paintings by Italian artist Alberto
Magnelli (1888–1971).
*Place de la Libération. Tel: 04 93 64 16
05. Open: mid-June–mid-Sept,
Wed–Mon, 10am–noon & 2–6pm; mid-
Sept–mid-June, Wed–Mon, 10am–noon
& 2–5pm. Admission charge.*

Musée National Picasso

In 1952 Picasso decorated the walls of
Vallauris's 13th-century Romanesque
chapel (in the château's courtyard) with
a huge War and Peace tableau.
*Place de la Libération. Tel: 04 93 64 16 05;
www.musee-picasso-vallauris.fr. Open:
mid-June–mid-Sept, Wed–Mon, 10am–
noon & 2–6pm; mid-Sept–mid-June,
Wed–Mon, 10am–noon & 2–5pm.
Admission charge.*

Musée de la Poterie

Pottery demonstrations take place in
this faithful reconstruction of an early
20th century workshop.

Rue Sicard. Tel: 04 93 64 66 51. Open: Mon–Sat, 2–6.30pm. Admission charge. Vallauris is in the hills between Cannes and Antibes.

Vence

After its high-flying neighbour, St-Paul-de-Vence (*see p114*), Vence brings you back down to earth. There is nothing particularly arty about Vence, a town that is too busy serving its resident population of 14,000. The thousands who have moved here in recent decades, attracted by the gentle climate and the booming sun-belt industries, have created something of an urban sprawl around the old town. But they have also brought a vitality and renewed purpose to Vence, without damaging the inherent charm of its historic centre.

A ring of medieval ramparts and gateways protected Vieux Vence (Old Vence). Much of the defence remains, most notably at the Porte du Peyra, a 15th-century fortified gate with 17th-century additions. Place du Peyra and place Clemenceau are charming tree-shaded open areas. The latter gives access to the former cathedral, dating from the 10th century but incorporating Roman fragments and later additions. The latest of all, in the baptistery, is the most striking: a mosaic by Marc Chagall depicting Moses in the bulrushes.

The town has strong links with many painters and writers. In the 1920s it became an artistic haven, attracting the likes of Gide, Dufy and DH Lawrence, who died here in 1930 of tuberculosis.

Chapelle du Rosaire

Henri Matisse designed and decorated this chapel between 1947 and 1951. The stark use of colour in his bold black-and-white ceramic murals – a surprise to many – finds a counterpoint in his marvellous stained-glass windows.
466 avenue Henri-Matisse. Tel: 04 93 58 03 26. Open: Mon, Wed & Sat, 2–5.30pm; Tue & Thur, 10–11.30am & 2–5.30pm. Other times by prior arrangement. Closed: Nov. Free admission. Vence is 24km (15 miles) west of Nice.

Shaded cafés in the old town of Vence provide a pleasant lunch-stop

Alpes-de-Haute-Provence

Provence's away-from-it-all *département* – and its least populated – is the meeting ground between Mediterranean and Alpine influences. Pastoral foothills in the south eventually rise into rocky mountain ranges, snowcapped for much of the year. Apart from developments along the Durance Valley, the Alpes-de-Haute-Provence is largely unaffected by change. Its rugged character and robust, grey-stoned mountain villages make it the least Provençal of the region's five *départements*.

Castellane, dominated by a massive chapel-crowned limestone rock

Castellane

Castellane's location at the eastern approach of the Grand Cañon du Verdon (*see pp128–9*) guarantees a healthy number of summer visitors. Its market square, place Marcel-Sauvaire, is set against a backdrop of steep hills. The steepest of all is the huge rocky outcrop, looming over the town, which is topped by the little pilgrimage chapel of Notre-Dame-du-Roc. The 18th-century chapel is a 30-minute walk along a path that passes the Tour Pentagonale, a five-sided fortified tower that was part of the town's medieval defences.

Castellane is an excellent centre for outdoor pursuits in and around the Grand Cañon, with equipment shops and agencies covering the whole sporting spectrum, from mountain biking to white-water rafting.
Castellane is 63km (39 miles) northwest of Grasse.

Digne-les-Bains

Digne's famous spa is hidden in a secluded, wooded valley a few kilometres from the centre. Whilst the *thermes* have an ongoing air of prosperity, the town itself shows a few signs of neglect. The cathedral, a grim-looking hulk enlivened by a tall campanile, needs some care and attention. The open spaces of place Général-de-Gaulle are much more visitor-friendly, though lacking the animated atmosphere of other French towns. But do not be discouraged by these negatives. Digne, which enjoys a beautiful, mountain-ringed location, is a restrained place with an understated charm typical of many spa towns.

Musée Alexandra David-Néel

The house of the fiercely individualistic Alexandra David-Néel recalls her fascination with all things Tibetan.
*27 avenue du Maréchal-Juin.
Tel: 04 92 31 32 38. www.alexandra-david-neel.org. Open (guided tours only): July–Sept, daily, 10am–6pm; Oct–June, daily, 10am–5pm. Admission charge.*

Alpes-de-Haute-Provence

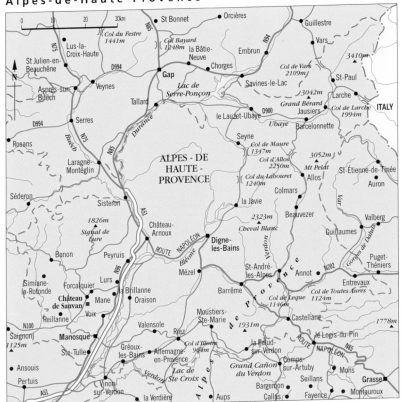

Musée Gassendi

Archaeology, art and natural history are all covered here.

64 boulevard Gassendi. Tel: 04 92 31 45 29. Open: Apr–Sept, Tue–Sun, 11am–7pm; Oct–Mar, Tue–Sun, 1.30–5.30pm. Admission charge.

Digne-les-Bains is 117km (73 miles) northwest of Grasse.

Entrevaux

The town makes no secret of its strategic importance. You enter by crossing the fairy-tale Porte Royale, a remarkable fortified bridge over the River Var. But that is just the beginning, for the citadel that fulfils the serious defensive role is perched high on a rock above the rooftops, an eyrie from which it keeps a threatening, all-seeing eye on the valley.

The original fortification was strengthened in the late 17th century by Vauban, Louix XIV's military architect, to defend this frontier town in France's disputes with Savoy. The only way up is along a zigzagging pathway cut into the rock. If you can't face the climb, then content yourself with Entrevaux's 17th-century cathedral which is built into the town's street-level defences. As a respite from Entrevaux's overpoweringly medieval air, you can retreat into the decidedly 20th-century little museum that celebrates the motor car.

Musee de la Poudriére open: daily, 9am–6pm. Further details from the Office de Tourisme (tel: 04 93 05 46 73) and Town Hall (tel: 04 93 05 40 04).

Entrevaux is on the N202, 72km (45 miles) northwest of Nice.

Forcalquier

This unexpectedly engaging small town lies at the heart of Provence between the Mediterranean and the Alps, a hilly, sunny area in which olive and beech trees grow side by side. Forcalquier has all the trappings of a long history – a ruined hilltop citadel, cathedral, wealth of other religious sites, Romanesque monuments, weathered Renaissance façades – but little of the fame enjoyed by other heritage-rich towns.

The town's Golden Age was in early medieval times when the counts of Forcalquier created an independent state which lasted for over a century. Unlike places such as Aix, in which every ancient feature is assiduously cherished, Forcalquier is not meticulous about preserving its past.

If you prefer your historic sites in their original state, then this is the place for you. Dominating place du Bourguet, the central square, is the former Cathédrale Notre-Dame, a large complex dating from the early 12th century. Opposite is the Couvent de la

The medieval fortified town of Entrevaux commands the River Var

Visitation, an old convent and chapel of delicately carved stonework that have unceremoniously been converted into a town hall, museum – and cinema!

The old town lies behind the cathedral, an area of 13th- to 18th-century houses that look their age. Place St-Michel's 16th-century fountain has an explicit carving demonstrating that medieval sexual practices in France deserve a mention in the *Kama Sutra*.

A short distance south of Forcalquier are two interesting places to visit – the Château de Sauvan and the Observatoire de Haute-Provence.

Château de Sauvan
This opulent 18th-century château, set in splendid grounds, looks like a refugee from the Loire Valley.
About 7km (4 miles) south of Forcalquier on the N100. Tel: 04 92 75 05 64.
Open for guided tour only: July–Aug, daily (except Sat), at 3.30pm; Sept–June, Thur & Sun, 3.30pm. Admission charge.

Couvent des Cordeliers
Forcalquier's 13th-century Franciscan monastery preserves its scriptorium, library, monastic hall and terraces.
Boulevard des Martyrs de la Résistance. Tel: 04 92 75 25 19. Open: for exhibitions daily, 10am–2pm & 4–7pm. Admission charge.

Musée de Salagon
A museum housed in a medieval priory with gardens of rich botanical interest attached.
Prieuré de Salagon, Mane (3.5km/2 miles southwest of Forcalquier). Tel: 04 92 75 70 50; www.musee-de-salagon.com. Open:

Forcalquier's church of Notre Dame de Provence was once a cathedral

Feb–Apr & Oct, daily, 2–5pm; May & Sept, daily, 10am–12.30pm & 2–6.30pm; June–Aug, daily, 10am–7.30pm; Nov & Dec, Sun only, 2–5pm. Admission charge.

Observatoire de Haute-Provence
The National Centre for Scientific Research sited its observatory here because of the area's clear skies and lack of industrial pollution.
Accessible via St-Michel l'Observatoire off the N100 southwest of Forcalquier. Tel: 04 92 76 69 69; www.centre-astro.fr. Open: Apr–Sept, Wed, 2–4pm; Oct–Mar, Wed only, one session at 3pm.

Forcalquier is 83km (52 miles) northeast of Aix-en-Provence.

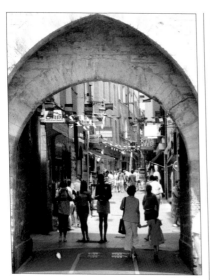

Walk under the arch of the Porte Saunerie to enter the old town of Manosque

Centre Jean Giono
1 boulevard Elémir-Bourges.
Tel: 04 92 70 54 55.
www.centrejeangiono.com. Open: Apr–Sept, Tue–Sun, 9.30am–noon & 2–6pm; rest of the year, Tue–Sat 2–6pm. Admission charge.

Grand Cañon du Verdon
See pp128–9.

Manosque

This bustling town is set on a hillside above the wide Durance Valley. Not so long ago, only 5,000 people lived here: that figure has now quadrupled. A strategic location, good communications by autoroute, a nearby nuclear research centre and an enviable climate have turned Manosque into the archetypal Provençal boom town. Signs of affluence are everywhere: in the neatly refurbished streets, the solidly middle-income shops and the well-dressed populace.

Manosque's focus of interest lies within the relatively small area of the old town, defined by a circular one-way traffic system. You can enter on foot through Porte Saunerie, a tall, fortified gateway that looks like a disembodied castle tower. A short distance along the pedestrianised rue-Grande is a plaque announcing the birthplace, on 30 March 1895, of writer Jean Giono (1895–1970), who wrote about the people and places of this part of Provence (*see p104*). A little further along rue-Grande is the **Église St-Sauveur** with a handsome, plain façade and ornate wrought-iron campanile (a bell cage, built to withstand the *mistral* wind, which you see on churches and monuments all across Provence).

This is a town that rewards aimless wandering. You will come across many pleasing details: the shady fountains, the decorative touches in the mellow stonework, the beautifully carved doorways (look out especially for the Renaissance carvings on the portal of Manosque's other church, the **Église Notre-Dame-de-Romigier**).

Manosque is 50km (31 miles) northeast of Aix-en-Provence.

Le froid ('Cold') statue in Manosque

Santons

Folk art and religious faith come together in Provence in the Nativity scenes that occupy proud places in the home at Christmas time. The figures, known as *santons* (little saints), are made of baked clay formed from plaster-cast moulds. They are painted in meticulous detail with acrylics and range from thimble-size to doll-size.

A town in miniature

These crèches are unique, for they contain not only the biblical figures of Jesus, Mary, Joseph, shepherds and Wise Men, but also a supporting cast representing people in a 19th-century Provençal town. Wearing clothes of that period, the *santons* depict a cross-section of society: farmers, fishermen, shopkeepers, teachers, businessmen, priests, and so on. There are sometimes more than a hundred figures on display, as well as intricately fashioned models of stone houses surrounding the stable. Twigs of rosemary and thyme depict trees, while hillsides are made out of pebbles and moss.

Spreading custom

The custom began in Marseille early in the 19th century, when the original *santonniers* (*santon* makers) modelled their figurines on the village characters portrayed in the Nativity plays known as *pastorales* and the ingenious *crèches parlantes* ('talking cribs' with speaking marionettes). The custom spread to neighbouring towns and villages and has since become a popular Provençal tradition. Marseille and the nearby city of Aix-en-Provence are still the *santon*-making centres of Provence, and a great *santon* fair is held in Marseille for two weeks each winter. Although especially linked to the festive season, *santons* can be bought at craft shops and fairs in Provence at any time of the year.

Colourful *santons* in 19th-century dress, sold as souvenirs nowadays

Moustiers-Ste-Marie

Moustiers is invariably criticised for being a tourist trap. This is unfair. The criticisms, one suspects, are based on pure aesthetics: whereas some places along the coast are a lost cause, Moustiers could be even more attractive without the souvenir and gift shops.

Its location is breath-taking. The village is built into the side of a V-shaped ravine split by a rushing watercourse, a fairy-tale setting. In the town you will find pottery shops … and pottery shops … and pottery shops. Moustiers pottery has been famous for centuries. After a spell in the doldrums, the industry revived in the 1930s and now makes a thriving living off its glazed decorative ware.

Another reason for the village's popularity is its location at the western gateway to the Grand Cañon du Verdon (*see pp128–9*). In summer, congestion is a problem. The sensible thing to do is to come early or late in the day – or, better still, in the spring or autumn.

Exploration is a delight when you have the place to yourself. The pretty cobbled square above the church leads to a steep pathway that climbs high up the side of the ravine to

ROUTE NAPOLÉON

After escaping from the island of Elba in March 1815, Napoléon landed at Golfe-Juan, marching northwards with a small band of followers to reclaim Paris. His route took him through Cannes, Mouans-Sartoux, St-Vallier-de-Thierry, Escragnolles and Castellane, where he crossed the Verdon by the now disused stone bridge. He was hardly greeted with open arms, and had to avoid Grasse, continuing on through the hills and mountains on stony, obscure tracks. It was not until he reached Gap that he began to regain some of his hero status.

His march through the mountains is commem-orated by the winding N85, now known as the Route Napoléon, built in the 1930s.

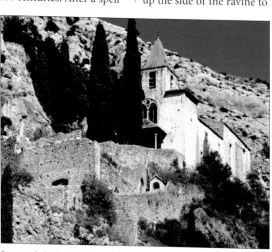

Spectacularly situated Moustiers has produced fine ceramics for centuries

a second religious site, the 12th-century **Chapelle Notre-Dame-de-Beauvoir**. Higher still, suspended on a 227-m (745-ft) long chain, is a famous curiosity – a man-sized star, supposedly placed there by a knight returning from the Crusades (the existing version, it should be pointed out, is 1957-vintage).

Musée de la Faïence (Pottery Museum)
Exhibits trace the history of Moustiers pottery.
Place du Presbytère.
Tel: 04 92 74 61 64 (Office de Tourisme).
Open: Apr–Oct, Wed–Mon, 9am–noon, 2–6pm. Admission charge.

Moustiers-Ste-Marie is 48km (30 miles) south of Digne-les-Bains.

Riez

Neighbouring Moustiers-Ste-Marie grabs all the attention, leaving Riez to its fate as an obscure country town. The visitors who do come – accidentally or otherwise – will discover a great deal of antiquity, presented without any of the usual fuss or flourish. Riez was an important meeting of the ways for the Romans. Four Roman columns, the remnants of a temple, stand like a piece of surreal art in a field on the outskirts of town. The original Roman settlement was on the hill of Mont St-Maxime above, the site of a 17th-century chapel and a good viewpoint across the surrounding lavender fields.

Further echoes of Riez's former – and now faded – glory can be traced amongst the rich Renaissance façades along Grand-Rue, the early Christian baptistery next to the excavated site of the cathedral, and the grandly proportioned Hôtel de Ville (Town Hall), originally an episcopal palace.
Riez is 42km (26 miles) south of Digne-les-Bains.

Sisteron

You need not be a military historian to understand Sisteron's strategic value. It grew up at a point where the Durance Valley funnels into a narrow defile between two enormous outcrops. Surmounting the western rock is an awesome, grey-stone citadel, guardian of a crucial gateway into Provence from the Alps.

The medieval citadel stands on a site that has been fortified for thousands of years. From the summit, high above the single bridge across the river, the citadel's grey mass is mirrored by the outcrop of Rocher de la Baume opposite.

Below, tall dwellings line a maze of narrow streets known locally as *andrônes*. Instead of having the usual stone facing, they are rendered as protection against the cold draught from the Alps, giving Sisteron a robust mountain character rather than a sybaritic Mediterranean warmth.

Citadelle

Before it suffered Allied bombing in 1944, this towering fortress-cum-prison, built between the 13th and 17th centuries, was even more impressive.
Tel: 04 92 61 27 57. Open: summer, daily, 9am–7pm; winter, daily, 9am–5pm. Closed: Dec–Mar. Admission charge.

Sisteron is 48km (30 miles) south of Gap.

Tour: Grand Cañon du Verdon

Some much-touted natural spectacles prove to be an anti-climax. The Grand Cañon du Verdon is categorically not amongst them. This first-division site is, in places, literally breathtaking. A giant slash cut deep into the earth's crust with heart-stopping 800-m (2,625-ft) drops and awesome vistas, this is one of the not-to-be-missed places on any visit to Provence. A road runs right around the canyon on both sides, thus allowing a convenient circular car tour of the entire spectacle. That is the good news.
With stops, the tour will take all day.

The bad news is its popularity. In summer, this route is a busy one. You will have to keep a wary eye not only on the road, which skirts some truly fearsome cliff edges, but also on other sightseeing motorists. Far better to come in the quieter autumn or spring, when you will have this stunning phenomenon almost entirely to yourself. You should also bear in mind that petrol stations in this remote corner are few and far between.

From Moustiers-Ste-Marie (see p126) take the D957 south, turning left on to the D19, which winds its way up through scrubland to Aiguines.

1 Aiguines

The pretty hilltop village of Aiguines enjoys wonderful views westwards to the Lac de Ste-Croix – a huge man-made sheet of unnaturally blue water fed by the River Verdon – and the strange,

flat-topped plateau above it.
From Aiguines, the serpentine road climbs up the Col d'Illoire for the first glimpse into the achingly deep canyon.

2 Corniche Sublime

The Col d'Illoire marks the start of the Corniche Sublime, which runs along the canyon's southern rim. Mossy, sheer-sided cliffs line the walls of a narrow defile carved by the Verdon. Along the corniche are noticeboards giving details of walks of different lengths and gradations into the canyon. Please note that some of these paths are very steep, so choose your trail carefully.
Beyond Les Cavaliers the road enters the Tunnels de Fayet, then crosses the River Artuby, a tributary of the Verdon. A short distance after the bridge, stop off at the Balcons de la Mescla, a viewpoint overlooking a great loop in the Verdon. This is your last glimpse of the gorge and river on the southern leg of the journey.

Follow the D71 eastwards, turning left along the D90 towards Trigance, then left on the D955 for Pont de Soleils and the D952. Here, you can take a detour east to Castellane (see p120). A few kilometres west of Pont de Soleils on the D952, take a short detour after the tunnel to the Belvédère du Couloir Samson, which ends in a deep cleft beside the rushing Verdon. Return to the D952 for the lofty viewpoint of 783-m (2,569-ft) high Point Sublime. Continue westwards, turning left along the Route des Crêtes (D23).

A dizzying look down into the mighty Grand Cañon du Verdon

3 Route des Crêtes

By now you may be tempted to miss the D23 loop, having had a surfeit of viewpoints. But on this tour, the best is kept for last. The Route des Crêtes is a must, eclipsing even the Corniche Sublime. There are so many breathtaking *belvédères* – and hair-raising hairpin bends – that it is

impossible to describe them all (the 1,285-m (4,216-ft) high **Belvédère du Pas de la Baou** is particularly stunning). *Rejoin the D952 at La Palud-sur-Verdon, passing the point where the river suddenly escapes from the canyon into the lake on the return to Moustiers.*

Wildlife

The abundance of plant and animal life in Provence makes it a fascinating destination for naturalists. Wild rosemary and thyme grow on the pine-scented hillsides, while

pyramidal cypress trees bring a darker, more dramatic accent of green to the surroundings. Vines flourish on sunny, stony slopes and plains, sometimes sharing a valley floor or hillside with olive groves.

Another distinct feature of Provence is the *garrigue* or *maquis*, names given to the dense undergrowth of stunted, hard-leafed evergreens, shrubs and bushes that harbour a wealth of animals. Orchids thrive in some areas, and edible fungi include truffles, which are gathered in Vaucluse with the aid of trained dogs. Palms and cacti add to the variety the region holds for visitors from cooler climes.

The flowers of Provence attract butterflies of many species, and moths are to be found in profusion. Summer visitors among the bird population include the gaudy bee-eater, which feeds off insects it catches on the wing. The Camargue is a world-class nature reserve renowned for its exceptional birdlife, which includes pink flamingoes, marsh- and seabirds, waterfowl and birds of prey. Look out for egrets, perched on the back of cattle, feeding off the Camargue's itchy insect life.

Wild boars find shelter in the protective *garrigue*. Together with quails, pheasants, partridges – and practically anything else with a pair of wings or four legs – they attract the attention of the hunting-mad Provençals outside the protected areas. Other Provençal residents include beavers, many reptiles (tortoises, snakes, lizards) and even a few golden eagles in the remoter mountains.

You will not have to look too hard to find the cicada with its insistent click, a creature synonymous with a hot Provençal summer. And do not be too concerned if you see a scorpion scurrying out from under a rock – the French variety will, at worst, give you something like a wasp sting.

Exotic flamingoes and the distinct breed of white horses are some of the abundant wildlife to be seen in the region

Getting away from it all

'It is to be tranquilly overwhelmed to see the Mediterranean just before dawn, stretching out beneath your windows. There will be the grey satin of the sea, the mountains behind, the absolutely convincing outline of Reinach's Greek villa at the end of Beaulieu Point. And the memory of Greek gods . . .'

FORD MADOX FORD
It Was the Nightingale 1933

Provence has a lot to offer the naturalist

Ardèche gorges

The gorges of the Ardèche get you away from Provence rather than away from it all. Only a short distance across the Rhône Valley from the Vaucluse, it would be pedantic in the extreme to ignore these gorges, one of the great natural wonders of France, even though they are technically outside the area. The gorges were formed by the River Ardèche, which has cut a deep channel through the limestone strata of a high plateau. They lie between Vallon-Pont-d'Arc (the main 'resort' town for the gorges) and **St-Martin-d'Ardèche** (a smaller tourist centre across the river from the cliff-top fort at Aiguèze). The as-the-crow-flies distance between the two is a mere 18km (11 miles), which almost trebles when you follow the serpentine road that imitates the convoluted, looping progress of the river.

There are two ways of seeing the gorges. You can drive the corniche road, the D290, which has many spectacular viewpoints along the way. Access by foot into the deepest recesses of the gorge is impossible from these high *belvédères*: you will have to be content to stand and gaze. The only easy access to river level is at the beginning and end of the gorges, where there are popular swimming and sunbathing 'beach' areas.

The second method, by canoe, is far more rewarding. Canoe hire is extremely well organised from the two main centres, Vallon-Pont-d'Arc and St-Martin, with transport laid on for the outward or return leg of the journey. Make sure that you get good advice about the different sections of the river. Some parts are calm and easy, so little or no previous experience is required (though you must be able to swim!). Others, involving rapids, should only be tackled by the more experienced. You will be given tuition if necessary and full equipment (life jackets, waterproof containers, etc). Canoes can be hired for anything from half a day to two days (overnight camping is permitted). Water conditions range from calm to fast-flowing. The best time for novices is between June and August, when conditions are at their best and other canoeists are present in reassuringly high numbers. As an alternative to the do-it-yourself approach, there are trips piloted by experienced boatmen (ask at Vallon-Pont-d'Arc's Office de Tourisme for details, *tel: 04 75 88 04 01*).

The journey starts at Vallon-Pont-d'Arc. Within a few kilometres you will come across the Ardèche's most-photographed feature, the famous **Pont-d'Arc**, a natural arch 34m (112ft) high and 59m (194ft) wide (also accessible from the D290). From here, the river is shut away for 30km (19 miles), looping and meandering within an inaccessible chasm lined with towering walls of rock rising to 300m (984ft).

The D290 runs along the northern rim of the gorges. Its most spectacular section is the **Haute Corniche** (High Corniche) about two-thirds of the way along to St-Martin. **Belvédère de la Madeleine**,

a short walk from the road, and the roadside **Belvédère de la Cathédrale** are tremendous viewpoints overlooking the highest part of the gorge.

Aven d'Orgnac

This is one of Europe's finest showcaves, and also houses a prehistory museum. *Near Barjac south of the gorges. Tel: 04 75 38 65 10. Open: Apr, May, June & Sept, daily, 10am–5.30pm; July–Aug till 6.30pm; Feb & Mar, daily, 10.30am–noon & 2–4.45pm; Oct–Nov, daily, 9.30am–noon & 2–5.15pm. Guided tours only. Admission charge.*

Canoe hire

There are many operators offering more or less the same service. Here are two:
Alpha Bateaux *Pierre Peschier, route des Gorges, Vallon-Pont-d'Arc. Tel: 04 75 88 08 29.*
Aventure Canoes *Place du Marché, Vallon-Pont-d'Arc. Tel: 04 75 37 18 14.*

The clifftop fort at Aiguèze stands above the River Ardèche

Aven de Marzal

This attraction offers tours of an underground cave system, museum and prehistoric 'zoo' with life-size dinosaurs. *Near St-Remèze, north of the gorges. Tel: 04 75 04 12 45. Open: Apr–Sept, daily, 9am–6pm; July–Aug, daily, 10am–7.30pm. Admission charge.*

Abbaye du Thoronet

This secluded abbey lies hidden in the Forêt de la Darboussière (Darboussière Forest) north of the A8 autoroute in the Haut-Var. Together with the Abbaye de Sénanque (*see p37*) and the Abbaye de Silvacane (*see p49*), it is one of the 'three Provençal sisters' founded by the Cistercians in the 12th century. The earliest – and possibly the finest – of the three, it bears all the hallmarks of the Cistercians' ascetic approach. Its austere simplicity combined with harmonious proportions gives it a rare beauty. *The most straightforward approaches are either via Brignoles in the west or Draguignan in the east. Tel: 04 94 60 43 90. Open: summer, Mon–Sat, 10am–6.30pm, Sun, 10am–noon & 2–7pm; winter, daily, 10am–1pm & 2–5pm. Admission charge.*

Massif des Maures

If you want to escape from the crowded coast between Hyères and St-Tropez, then head inland into the densely wooded, sparsely populated hills of the Massif des Maures, the oldest mountain range in Provence. Its name derives from the Provençal *maouro*, used to describe this upland's dark cover of cork oak,

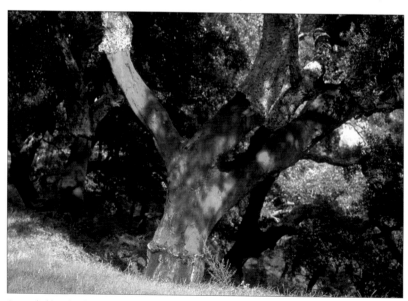

A grand old cork-oak tree

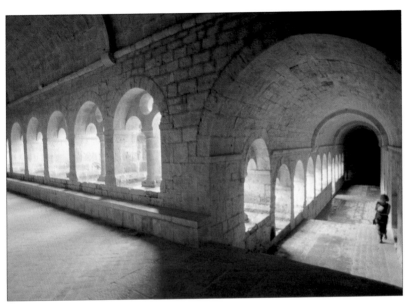

Long silent corridors of the Abbaye du Thoronet

chestnut and pine. There are a few tortuous, twisting roads through the mountains, though the Maures – which rise to over 700m (2,297ft) – are best explored on foot (the cross-country GR9 path takes in most of the high ridges).

La Garde-Freinet, the tiny 'capital' of the Maures, was France's main cork-producing town in the 19th century. It still makes a living from the local cork oak, though nowadays it has diversified into cork craft ornaments for tourists. Its ruined medieval castle marks the site of an earlier stronghold occupied by the feared Saracens.

To the southwest, in the heart of the Maures, is the ancient village of Collobrières. Confectionery made from sweet chestnuts has now replaced its cork industry. A mountain pass

northwards climbs to **Notre-Dame-des-Anges**, a pilgrimage site almost at the summit of the Maures, which enjoys predictably panoramic views.

Sweet chestnuts for sale in the Massif des Maures

The limestone hills of the Luberon provide diverse and beautiful landscapes

Montagne de Lure

This mountain, a near sister to the slightly higher Mont Ventoux (*see pp46–7*), rises to 1,826m (5,991ft) above Sisteron and the Durance Valley. Not as well-served by roads (nor as heavily featured in guidebooks) as Mont Ventoux, its wooded slopes and barren summit offer a real chance of escape.

The mountain can be approached from north or south. For a north-south tour, leave Sisteron on the N85, taking the D946 through the pretty Jabron Valley. Then turn left on to the D53 (closed in winter), which winds along the base of a natural amphitheatre for about 5km (3 miles) before it starts the ascent of Lure's forested slopes.

Aire de St-Robert is an attractive picnic area, the starting point for a number of woodland walks. From here, the road surface becomes poorer for a few kilometres, though the views soon make the effort worthwhile: through the trees you will catch glimpses of the snowcapped Alps as well as the Forêt Domaniale du Jabron, which covers Lure's thickly wooded foothills.

At the 1,597-m (5,240-ft) high Col du Pas de la Graille, trees give way to patchy moorland, bare rock and even better views. If you are feeling energetic, you can park the car here and follow a footpath the final few kilometres to the summit of Signal de Lure.

The summit, like that of Ventoux, bristles with strange-looking telecommunications equipment. A dizzy 360-degree panorama seems to encompass most of southern France, from the jagged Alps to the plateaux and plains leading down to the coast.

The descent of the mountain is on the wider D113 to sleepy St-Etienne (nervous drivers might prefer to go up as well as down on this road).

Parc Naturel Régional du Luberon

The Luberon Regional Natural Park, bounded in the south by the Durance River and in the north by the beginnings of the Vaucluse Plateau, is a 60-km (37-mile) long chain of mountains rising to over 1,100m (3,609ft). The park consists of two parts: the Petit Luberon in the west near Cavaillon, a rugged area of gorges and ravines, and the higher Grand Luberon between Apt and Manosque in the east.

In the hierarchy of protected areas in France, a Regional Natural Park comes second to a National Park. The Luberon was declared a Regional Park in 1977 because of the special nature of its landscapes and local traditions. Unlike a National Park, where preservation of a wilderness area is paramount, a Regional Park attempts to balance conservation with appropriate sustainable commercial activities, including tourism.

In many ways, the Luberon takes its character from its villages, which are mostly strung out below its long spine of mountains. Human settlement, as much as natural forces, has shaped the Luberon's beautiful landscapes. Its hilltop villages (familiar to readers of Peter Mayle's *A Year in Provence*) are surrounded by vast patches of cultivated land, its higher pastures are tended by sheep farmers, and its ochre cliffs have been mined for dye.

The Luberon's fractured landscapes of high limestone cliffs, scrub, shrub and forest display an absolutely amazing diversity. Sunny south-facing slopes are clothed in an aromatic Mediterranean vegetation, while oaks grow along its cooler, more humid northern escarpment. Diversity is the keynote here, for the Luberon's rich flora and fauna include holm and downy oak, cedar, pine, cypress, rosemary, honeysuckle, lavender, eagle, owl, wild boar and beaver.

Full information on the park, including details of walking and cycle routes, is available at the Maison du Parc Naturel Régional du Luberon in Apt (*see p23*). Pages 24–5 feature a car tour of the Petit Luberon.

Parc National du Mercantour

In terms of outright environmental protection, this National Park is one notch up on the Luberon Regional Park. The Mercantour, roughly 90km by 30km (56 miles by 19 miles), runs close to the French/Italian border more or less from Sospel to Barcelonnette, embracing big-league mountains consistently in the 2,500–3,000m (8,200–9,850ft) range. Most of the park lies in the Alpes-Maritimes, with a small northern section in the Alpes-de-Haute-Provence.

Exploration of this challenging wilderness should not be taken lightly. Walkers should always expect the worst: parts of the park have a long, snowy winter that can last from October to June. Even in summer nothing is predictable, for weather conditions can change alarmingly in a short space of time and from valley to valley.

The Mercantour was Italian territory until after World War II, when it was ceded to France and became a nature reserve. Its highest mountain is Mont Pelat, a 3,051-m (10,010-ft) peak that rises above Lac d'Allos, a mountain lake itself at over 2,200m (7,218ft) and accessible by road from Allos. This northern corner of the park also contains the memorable mountain road over the 2,802-m (9,193-ft) high Col de la Bonette, which drops down into the Tinée Valley.

However, the Mercantour's acknowledged centrepiece lies further southeast at the **Val des Merveilles**. The only access to this remote valley is by foot. From St-Dalmas-de-Tende on the N204 north of Saorge (*see pp114–15*) the D91 leads west for about 8km (5 miles) to Les Mesches, starting point for a 10-km (6-mile) footpath into this dramatic valley with its mysterious Bronze Age rock carvings.

The Mercantour's wildlife could fill a book. More than half of the 4,000 species of wildflowers growing in France are found here, including rare saxifrage, lily and orchid. The park, of course, is the perfect habitat for eagles, buzzards, falcons and kestrels. Other species at home here include chamois, ibex and wild boar.

Réserve Naturelle Géologique de Haute Provence

Eighteen separate sites centred around Digne-les-Bains were declared Nature Reserves in 1984 in an attempt to protect them from damage. The earth's geological record is contained within this spread of valuable sites, which

The Mercantour National Park

A fascinating ammonite fossil

stretches from near Castellane in the south to Barles in the north, a distance of about 50km (31 miles). They contain deposits of plant life, ammonite skeletons from the time when sea covered the Alps, even traces of bird footprints left some 30 million years ago.

Public access to the sites is controlled. Information on guided visits is available from the Centre de Géologie (open daily) at St-Benoît about 4km (2¹/₂ miles) from the centre of Digne on the D900. This is a research establishment with exhibition rooms open to the public. *Tel: 04 92 336 70 70. Open: Apr–June & Sept–Oct, daily, 9am–noon & 2–5.30pm (4.30pm on Fri); July–Aug, Mon–Fri, 9am–1pm & 2–7pm, Sat–Sun, 10.30am–12.30pm & 2–7pm; Nov–Mar, Mon–Fri, 9am–noon & 2–5.30pm.*

Tourtour

Tourtour is typical of the enchanting Provençal villages you invariably stumble across when you wander off the main highways. To find Tourtour, a

village in the empty northern spaces of the Haut-Var, take the D77 (off the D557 west of Draguignan), a road that winds up a beautiful wooded escarpment.

The village, a picturesque jumble of vaulted archways, wrought-iron balconies, ancient stone staircases and shadowy passageways – with a fountain at almost every corner – would by now have been buried in souvenir shops were it nearer to the coast. Tourtour's lack of pretension is summed up by the way in which its post office is housed in a 16th-century bastion complete with four enormous round corner towers. Although the village shows signs of infiltration by craft galleries and expensive eating places, they do not yet dilute a convincingly authentic atmosphere.

From the Église St-Denis, Tourtour's lofty location at over 600m (1,969ft) becomes apparent. The church occupies a splendid viewpoint looking southwards to the sea, a panorama fully explained by a helpful *table d'orientation.*

Flowers abound in the pretty and still unspoilt village of Tourtour

Shopping

Best buys in Provence are undoubtedly its local crafts and artefacts. You will not even have to go into a conventional shop for some things. Family potteries, for example, often sell their wares beside the road; sometimes you will find fields the size of football pitches stacked full of kitchenware, urns, plates and pots. At the other end of the spectrum are expensive craft shops and galleries. Some villages, especially the 'perched villages' in southern Provence, have been completely taken over by such shops.

Shop sign in Gourdon

Items on sale include the miniature figures known as *santons* (*see p125*), toilette products made from local lavender and herbs, a wide range of pottery, leatherwork, honey, hand-woven baskets and the brightly patterned fabrics of traditional Provençal design. The best – but most expensive – place for the latter is the Souleiado or les Olivades range of stores. You can buy the fabric in lengths or already made into dresses, shirts, scarves, tablecloths, etc. Some towns specialise in particular products. Grasse is famous for its perfume, Biot for its exquisite glassware, and Vallauris for its colourful pottery.

Where to shop

There seems to be a standard pattern to the larger Provençal towns. The town centre is reserved for the smaller shops, while on the outskirts are sprawling complexes that contain the hypermarkets, motor accessory stores, and the large do-it-yourself and furniture outlets. While the hypermarkets are short on ambience (basically they are huge, functional shopping sheds), they are extremely convenient. In addition to the vast supermarket that forms the core of the centre, you will also find a range of other shops – selling everything from sports goods to musical instruments – all under one roof.

Prices

Do not try to haggle over prices – bargaining will get you nowhere in Provence. The exception to this rule is the outdoor flea market or antique sale. Here you can often negotiate a reduction of the asking price.

VAT

The Value Added Tax in France, known as TVA (*taxe à la valeur ajoutée*), is incorporated in the price of almost every item or meal. It varies slightly according to the category of product but is most widely applied at the 18.6 per cent level. Visitors from non-EU countries may, in some cases, be eligible for a TVA refund if the goods are taken out of the country within 90 days of being purchased. To facilitate this process, some stores offer an 'export sales invoice' (*bordereau* in French), which you must complete to make the claim, and both goods and *bordereau* must be shown to customs officials at the port or airport of departure. Note that not all shops offer this service, and others impose a minimal expenditure for the extra paperwork.

Opening hours

Shop hours in France respect the sanctity of the midday meal. Apart from the big stores and supermarkets, most shops close between noon and 2pm, though in compensation many stay open until quite late (6 or 7pm). Many towns and villages observe half-day closing at some time during the week. Conventional 'high street' shops are closed on Sunday, though shops aimed at the visitor market – craft shops, galleries, etc – usually remain open, especially in the popular tourist areas.

SPECIALITY SHOPS

Aix-en-Provence

Paul Fouque
This leading maker of *santons* has a shop and workshop.
65 cours Gambetta. Tel: 04 42 26 33 38.
Souleiado
8 place Chapeliers. Tel: 04 42 26 23 08.

Arles

Les Olivades
10 boulevard des Lices. Tel: 04 90 93 53 70.
Souleiado
18 boulevard des Lices. Tel: 04 90 96 37 55.

Aubagne

Poterie Ravel
Since 1837 this pottery has made elegant terracotta pots and ceramics.
Avenue des Goums. Tel: 04 42 82 42 00;
www.poterie-ravel.com

Avignon

There are many small speciality shops in the maze of narrow streets off the main rue de la République. One of the city's most stylish and exclusive shopping streets is rue Joseph Vernet.

Eden Pearls
This jeweller specialises in precious stones and pearls.
23 rue du Vieux Sextier.
Tel: 04 90 82 55 27.
Souleiado
5 rue Joseph Vernet. Tel: 04 90 86 47 67.

Biot

La Verrière de Biot
Biot's distinctive bubbled glassware is made and sold here.
5 chemin des Combes. Tel: 04 93 65 03 00.

A boutique in Aix-en-Provence

Cannes

For the latest designer fashions with expense no object, there's none to beat the exclusive boutiques (Chanel, St-Laurent, etc) along Cannes' La Croisette. Rue d'Antibes and rue Meynadier are two other fashionable shopping streets.

Eze

Parfumerie Fragonard

This large perfumery, soap and cosmetics factory sells its products direct to the public.

On the Moyenne Corniche (middle coast road) between Nice and Monaco. Tel: 04 93 41 0505.

Fontaine-de-Vaucluse

Fabrication Artisanale de Papier, Vallis Clausa

Water-powered machinery helps in the production of handmade paper, which is used in a wide range of prints and maps.

Chemin de la Fontaine. Tel: 04 90 20 34 14; www.vallis-clausa.com

Grasse

You are spoilt for choice shopping for perfume – and you should be able to purchase the perfume at factory prices.

GLB Parfums

Zone Industriel Bois de Grasse, 175 boulevard Emmanuel Rouquier. Tel: 04 92 42 09 57.

Parfumerie Fragonard

20 boulevard Fragonard. Tel: 04 93 36 44 65. Also 2km (1¹/₄ miles) from the town centre on the route de Cannes. Tel: 04 93 40 12 04; www.fragonard.com

Parfumerie Galimard

73 route de Cannes. Tel: 04 93 09 20 00; www.galimard.com

Grasse's surrounding meadows yield the flowers for its perfume industry

Parfumerie Molinard
60 boulevard Victor-Hugo.
Tel: 04 93 36 01 62.

Marseille
Santons Marcel Carbonel
This shop and workshop, run by a
famous *santonnier*, also has a small
museum.
47 rue Neuve Ste-Catherine.
Tel: 04 91 54 26 58.
Souleiado
117 rue Paradis. Tel: 04 91 04 69 30.

Monaco
The best shopping areas are: the
cluster of streets in La Vieille-Ville; in
La Condamine, the pedestrian area
of rue Grimaldi and rue Princesse
Caroline; in Monte Carlo, in the
Centre Commercial La Métropole,
boulevard des Moulins and the
Galerie du Park-Pale in avenue de la
Costa; and in Fontvieille, the Centre
Commercial in avenue Prince-
Héreditaire Albert.

Nice
You will find most of the major stores
along avenue Jean-Médecin, the main
shopping thoroughfare, along avenue
de Verdun, and the more upmarket
Masséna quarter, a pedestrianised area
of chic boutiques.

Confiserie du Vieux Nice
Crystallised fruit is a speciality of Nice.
There are guided tours of this
confectionery, and a wide selection of
its colourful range of products.
14 quai Papacino.
Tel: 04 93 55 43 50.

Nîmes
Les Olivades
Specialists in Provençal fabrics.
4 place Maison Carrèe. Tel: 04 66 21 01 31.

St-Rémy-de-Provence
Les Olivades
Traditional Provençal fabrics – garments
and accessories.
Place de la Mairie. Tel: 04 90 92 00 80.
Souleiado
2 avenue de la Résistance.
Tel: 04 90 92 45 90.

Salon-de-Provence
Chocolaterie Le Nostradamus
Freshly made chocolates and sweets.
122 avenue 22 Août. Tel 04 90 53 13 97.

Séguret
M. Fournier
The shop is small, just like the miniature
santons it sells – but there is a wonderful
choice of items.
Rue Poternes. Tel: 04 90 46 91 35.

Tourrettes-sur-Loup
Confiserie des Gorges-sur-Loup
Sweet-making is elevated to a fine art at
this candied fruit factory and shop.
Le Pont du Loup.
Tel: 04 93 59 32 91.

Vallauris
Céramiques Natoli
This pottery shop also gives
demonstrations in pot-throwing as well
as selling its wares.
*Avenue Jérôme-Massier/boulevard des
deux Vallons.*
Tel: 04 93 63 90 14;
www.ceramiques-natoli.com

Finely crafted baskets for sale

MARKETS

Provence's open-air markets are as much a tourist attraction as its beautiful places and historic sites. All the big towns and many villages hold weekly – sometimes daily – markets. The streets are crammed full of stalls, and market-goers shuffle along in the sunshine as the mingling aromas of lavender, herbs, ripe cheese, olives, fresh fish and chicken roasting on a spit, waft through the crowds. The markets are the best free show in Provence. Stallholders tempt the passing crowds with invitations to sample their wares, and in summer a variety of street entertainers soon gather large audiences for impromptu performances of everything from organ grinding to juggling.

You can buy almost anything at a Provençal market. In addition to the cheese, olive, bread, fish, fruit, vegetable, meat and flower stalls, there are large mobile shops that open up to reveal shoes, clothes, toys, hunting gear and gardening equipment.

Please note that, in most cases, the markets are mornings only. By noon, the stallholders are beginning to shut up shop and make for home or the nearest café.

Aix-en-Provence
Daily fruit and vegetable market (place Richelme); flower market on Tuesday, Thursday and Saturday (place de l'Hôtel-de-Ville); fruit, vegetable and herb market on Tuesday,

Thursday and Saturday (place des Prêcheurs); antiques market Tuesday, Thursday and Saturday mornings (place de Verdun).

Apt
Tuesday in Cours Lauze de Perrer.

Antibes
Daily general market (cours Masséna).

Arles
Wednesday and Saturday.

Avignon
Covered food market Tuesday to Sunday mornings (Les Halles). Flea market on Sunday (place des Carmes).

Barjols
Crafts Market Tuesday to Saturday.

Bédoin
Monday.

Cannes
Daily general market (Marché Forville). Bric-a-brac market on Saturday (allées de la Liberté).

Carpentras
Friday.

Châteauneuf-du-Pape
Friday.

Digne
Wednesday and Saturday.

Draguignan
Daily food market. Flea market first Saturday every month.

Fréjus
Wednesday and Saturday.

Gordes
Tuesday arts and crafts market.

Grasse
Provençal market Tuesday to Sunday.

L'Île-sur-la-Sorgue
Thursday. Antiques on Sunday.

Le Lavandou
Thursday.

Manosque
Saturday.

Marseille
Fish market daily except Sunday (quai des Belges).

Menton
Daily food market except Monday. Bric-a-brac market on Friday.

Monaco
Daily market (place d'Armes, Monte Carlo).

Moustiers-Ste-Marie
Friday.

Nice
Daily, except Sunday afternoon and Monday, all over the city. Bric-a-brac sold on Monday.

Nîmes
Monday flower and antiques market.

Orange
Bric-a-brac market on Thursday (Place des Cordeliers).

St-Rémy-de-Provence
Wednesday and Saturday.

St-Tropez
Tuesday and Saturday.

Stes-Maries-de-la-Mer
Monday and Friday.

Salon-de-Provence
Wednesday.

Sanary-sur-Mer
Daily market.

Sault
Wednesday.

Sisteron
Wednesday and Saturday.

Toulon
Daily general market.

Vaison-la-Romaine
Tuesday. Sunday morning in July and August.

A wonderful range of pottery

Crafts

The variety and quality of craftwork in Provence are evidence of a region in which folk art has achieved a high status. Craft traditions can be traced back at least as far as Roman times, for pottery workshops and kilns of the 1st century AD have been unearthed near Marseille.

Pottery and glass

The cheapest pottery produced today is called *terre rouge* after the reddish-brown colour it derives from the local red clay. Family workshops turn out jugs, bowls, pots and tiles, which are often sold at the roadside. The more decorative *faïence* style of pottery, first brought to France from Italy in the 16th century, has an enamel porcelain-like finish. Once found only in the homes of the wealthy, its appeal has since broadened considerably. *Grès* pottery, made from the grey clays of central France, lends itself to art pottery because of its hardness.

Another ancient craft has been brought to perfection in the town of Biot, where a unique method is employed to produce swirls of bubbles in clear or coloured blown glass.

Printed cottons

The vibrant printed cottons of Provence, known as *indiennes* because of their Indian influence, were first produced in the 17th century and have kept their strong appeal over the years. Traditionally they provided the humble shawl for generations of Provençal women, but they have now ventured up-market and are used for interior decoration, fashion garments and shirts. Their brilliant colours and sharply defined patterns capture the essence of life in this sun-soaked region.

Contemporary crafts

The crafts scene in Provence is by no means entirely rooted in traditional folk art. An influx of artists since the 1950s has extended the range of crafts from the earthy to the eclectic, as a visit to almost any gallery will demonstrate. Tradition now coexists with innovation across a whole spectrum of crafts, embracing everything including woven murals, wooden toys, soaps and alternative toiletries.

Fine pottery, printed cottons, Moustiers ceramics and Gourdon glassware: Provence's crafts are many and varied

Entertainment

Provence is essentially an open-air region. But that doesn't mean dedicated nightclubbers can't find the disco of their dreams. In northern Provence – apart from the main towns and cities – the sleepy, rural economy does not lend itself to frenetic entertainment when the lights go down. By 10pm, this part of Provence is soundly asleep. In the south, of course, it is just the opposite. Along the Riviera, the resorts buzz with life day and night.

Pavement cafés – cheerful and informal

CAFÉ SOCIETY

Everybody becomes part of the café society when in Provence. But, like societies the world over, there is a pecking order. You can enjoy a coffee or Coke and watch the world go by in the main square of a humble country town, or pose conspicuously in a celebrated watering place along the coast where the next table just might be occupied by someone famous.

And you will pay for the fame-by-association. Even in ordinary cafés, prices for drinks are high. In the top spots, they are quite outrageous.

Aix-en-Provence

Cours Mirabeau is the street for pavement cafés and promenading. Les Deux Garçons (*53 cours Mirabeau*), with its gilt panelling, mirrors and ambience of a more languorous age, attracts an arty crowd.

Arles

The delightful little square – straight out of Van Gogh – known as the place du Forum is lined with cafés. Bar Le Paris is

friendly. There are larger cafés along the boulevard des Lices.

Cannes

You will need a healthy bank balance to enjoy this resort to the full. Not only are the beaches and the film festival internationally famous; but one of the many attractive spots is the tea room, ice-cream parlour and restaurant of La Grande Brasserie, with its early 20th century decor, at 81 rue d'Antibes.

Monaco

Expect to pay whopping prices anywhere around Monte Carlo's place du Casino, the meeting place of the high-rollers. Prices are a little more sensible – but only just – in the old town of Monaco-Ville across the harbour.

St-Tropez

The cafés along the harbourside quai Jean-Jaurès are the places from which to see it all – the yachts, the parading crowds and the ostentatious displays of wealth.

CASINOS

Unsuccessful gamblers can blame it all on Monte Carlo, for it was here, in 1865, that the Riviera's first casino opened.

To add insult to injury, some casinos now impose an admission charge – so you have to pay in order to lose money! Many casinos restrict entry to those 21 and over.

Aix-en-Provence
Casino Municipal
21 avenue de l'Europe.
Tel: 04 42 59 69 00.

Antibes
La Siesta
Route du Bord de la Mer – direction Nice.
Tel: 04 93 33 31 31.

Cannes
Carlton Casino Club
58 boulevard La Croisette.
Tel: 04 93 68 00 33.
Casino Croisette
Jetée Albert-Edouard/La Croisette.
Tel: 04 93 38 12 11.
Grand Casino Riviera (Noga Hilton)
50 boulevard La Croisette.
Tel: 04 93 68 43 43.

Cassis
Casino Barrière de Cassis
Avenue du Professeur Leriche.
Tel: 04 42 01 78 32.

Juan-les-Pins
Eden Casino
Boulevard Baudoin.
Tel: 04 92 93 71 71.

Menton
Casino Barrière de Menton
Ave Félix-Fauré.
Tel: 04 92 10 16 16.

Monaco
Casino de Monte-Carlo
Place du Casino.
Tel: (377) 92 16 20 00.
Casino Sun
Monte-Carlo Grande Hotel, ave des Spélugues.
Tel: (337) 93 50 65 00.

Nice
Casino Ruhl
1 promenade des Anglais.
Tel: 04 97 03 12 22.

St-Raphaël
Grand Casino
Square de Gand.
Tel: 04 98 11 17 77.

Charles Garnier rebuilt the superb casino at Monte Carlo

DISCOS, CLUBS, BARS

Elegant piano bars, sophisticated night clubs, raucous discos – you name it and you'll find it. By their very nature, night-time venues tend to come and go as fashions change. Listed here are some of the well-known establishments.

Aix-en-Provence
Le Scat Club
Rue de la Verrerie.
Tel: 04 42 23 00 23.

Antibes/ Juan-les-Pins
Discothèque la Nuit
Avenue Gallicies.
Tel: 04 93 67 22 74.
La Siesta
Route du Bord de Mer in the direction of Nice.
Tel: 04 93 33 31 31.
Voom-Voom
1 boulevard de la Pinède.
Tel: 04 92 93 90 90.
Whisky à Go-go
Rue Jacques Leoneti.
Tel: 03 93 61 26 40.

Avignon
Auberge de la Treille
Piano jazz on summer evenings.
Chemin de l'ille Piot.
Tel: 04 90 16 46 20.
Le Rouge Gorge
A cabaret-restaurant going until 3am.

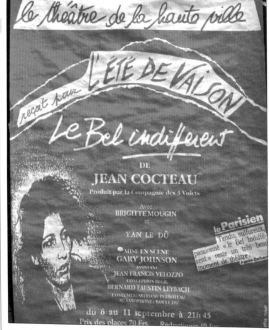

Plays by Jean Cocteau are always crowd pullers

1 bis rue de la Peyrolerie.
Tel: 04 90 14 02 54.

Cannes
Galaxy
Casino, Jetée Albert-Edouard/La Croisette.
Tel: 04 92 98 78 00.
Whisky à Go-go
115 avenue des Lérins.
Tel: 04 93 43 20 63.

Monaco
Le Sporting
Place du Casino, Monte Carlo.
Tel: (337) 92 16 20 00.

Nice
Casino Ruhl
1 promenade des Anglais.
Tel: 04 97 03 12 22.

Le Grande Escurial
One of the Cote d'Azur's largest discos.
29 rue Alphose Karr.
Tel: 04 93 82 37 66.
Le Relais
Hôtel Negresco, 37 promenade des Anglais.
Tel: 04 93 16 64 00.

St-Tropez
Le Bal
Résidence du Nouveau-Port.
Tel: 04 94 97 45 87.
Les Caves du Roy
Avenue Paul Signac.
Tel: 04 94 97 16 02.

THEATRES
A wide range of concerts, from opera to pop,

takes place in many different styles of venue throughout Provence. Some of the most atmospheric and popular performances are held in the open air of a summer's night in Provence's Roman amphitheatres.

Aix-en-Provence
Théâtre Jeu de Paume
17 rue Opéra.
Tel: 04 42 99 12 00.

Théâtre Ateliers
29 Place Miollis.
Tel: 04 42 38 10 45.

Arles
Théâtre Antique
Rue de la Calade/rue du Cloître.
Tel: 04 90 49 36 74.

Marseille
Opéra Municipal
1 place Reyer.
Tel: 04 91 54 94 15.

Monaco
Opéra de Monte-Carlo
The opera house is part of the casino.
Atrium du Casino, Place du Casino.
Tel: (337) 92 16 22 99.
Théâtre Princesse Grace
12 avenue d'Ostende.
Monte Carlo.
Tel: (337) 93 50 03 45.

Nice
Acropolis
Palais des Congrès,
1 Kennedy Esplanade.
Tel: 04 93 92 83 00.
Opéra de Nice
4 rue St-François-de-Paul.
Tel: 04 92 17 40 40.

Palais Nikaia
163 rue de Grenoble.
Tel: 04 92 29 31 29.
Théâtre de Nice
Esplanade Victoires.
Tel: 04 93 13 90 90.
Théâtre Municipal du Vieux Nice
4 rue St-Joseph.
Tel: 04 93 62 00 03.

Nîmes
Théâtre Antique
Boulevard des Arènes.
Tel: 04 66 21 82 56.

Orange
Théâtre Antique
Place des Frères-Mounet.
Tel: 04 90 34 70 88.

Toulon
Opéra de Toulon
7 rue Jean Racine.
Tel: 04 94 92 70 78.

Toulon's opera house has a beautifully decorated interior inspired by Charles Garnier

Property hunting

The anecdotal accounts of writer Peter Mayle of how he set up home in the Luberon were a catalyst in an already-growing trend for northerners to flock south in search of sun, beautiful scenery and *la belle vie française*. Thanks to the popularity of his books, a subtle shift in expatriate

focus took place from the historically popular Côte d'Azur and the Dordogne, to Provence and the Luberon. Today, some 20 years later, there are no bargains left; no small 'ruins in need of restoration', no barns or outhouses suitable for inexpensive modification.

Prices in Provence have rocketed, and the locals know full well the value of their property. Having said that, this does not mean that there is no property available: far

from it. There are probably far more property deals now than 20 years ago, but bargains are part of the past. To find a suitable second home, a house in which to live annually, or a working farm or *gîte*, requires considerable planning and probably as much – if not more – finance as a similar venture in Great Britain or other parts of Europe.

If you are not ready to take a research trip to Provence, then the internet is a good place to start looking at prices and types of property. Follow that up through contact with an accredited *agent immobilier* (estate agent). His or her fees, usually around six per cent, will already be included in the property price, and will cover showing you various properties, finding out about annual running costs, the *taxes foncières* and *taxes d'habitation* (the annual local taxes) and making appointments with a local *notaire* (notary), who will draw up and oversee the sale contract, and should undertake the basic searches. The notary's fee is between 6–10 per cent of the purchase cost (there is a prescribed sliding scale), and is paid over and above the purchase price.

The usual procedure is to make an offer for a property, and then, on acceptance by the vendor, pay the notary whilst signing a *compromis de vente*. A statutory period of time follows – usually six weeks – in which financing is organised and searches are undertaken before the finalisation of the purchase, the *acte de vente*, again requiring a signature before the notary.

Before rushing into a purchase, it is worth spending time in the area during the worst months of the year – even life in Provence is not always a bed of roses. Likewise, it is a good idea to overhaul one's linguistic skills – it is hard to make friends with the neighbours if all you can do is nod and smile. And dealing with the EDF (electricity board), France Telecom (the phone company), Générale des Eaux (water supplier), your new local bank, the local *mairie* (town hall), not to mention architects and suppliers, requires more than a basic command of the language to satisfactorily and speedily start up the running of a new home.

The warm, stone Provençal architecture, the charm of the area's beaches, its enviable climate and easy-going lifestyle have encouraged many expatriates to settle here

Camargue's horses are
trained for young riders

Children

Children who have had a surfeit of Provence's Roman remains and medieval sites deserve a break during the holiday. Attractions range from aquaparks to zoos.

Antibes
Marineland
This is a large attraction with aquariums and displays illustrating the sealife of the Mediterranean, video films, etc. The highlight of the visit is provided by the performing dolphins and killer whales. Other attractions grouped in the same location include an aqua-splash, butterfly jungle, farm park and adventure golf.
RN7-Antibes. Located just off RN7 3km (2 miles) east of Antibes and 12km (7 miles) west of Nice. Tel: 04 93 33 49 49; www.marineland.fr. Open: daily, 10am–4.30pm throughout the year. Admission charge.

Avignon
Le Parc du Soleil et du Cosmos
The park takes as its theme the discovery of the universe. Stars and planets speak directly to you (in French) in an imaginatively presented and educational attraction. 'An illustrated alphabet of space.'
Avenue Charles-de-Gaulle, 30133 Les Angles, Avignon. Tel: 04 90 25 66 82; www.parcducosmos.net. Open: for guided tours only Tue–Fri & Sun. Admission charge.

La Barben
Château de la Barben
Fully furnished château and beautiful gardens standing in 40 hectares (99 acres) of grounds with a large zoo – elephants, lions and other big cats, rhinos, snakes, crocodiles, birds, etc.
13330 La Barben, near Pélissanne just east of Salon-de-Provence. Tel: 04 90 55 19 12; www.zoolabarben.com. Open: 10am–8pm (ticket office closed weekdays in winter noon–1.30pm). Admission charge.

Bedarrides
Oxygène Aquarium Tropical
Three hundred kinds of tropical fish are displayed in this aquarium. You can even walk through a fascinating underwater 'tunnel'.
Between Orange and Avignon. 30 petite route de Sorgues, 84370 Bedarrides. Tel: 04 90 33 06 87. Open: Tue–Sat, 10am–noon & 2–7pm (till 6pm on Sun). Admission charge.

Châteauneuf-les-Martigues
Magicland
Wild West town with daily shows. Cowboy spectacles with stunt men and actors, train rides, puppet theatre and adventure playground. Picnic in the pine forest.
Châteauneuf-les-Martigues, north of Carry-le-Rouet, 25km (16 miles) west of the centre of Marseille on the A55. Tel: 04 42 79 86 90. Open: Mar–June, 10am–6pm; July–Aug, Sat & Sun, daily, 10am–6pm. Admission charge.

Cuges-les-Pins
OK Corral
Themed Wild West funfair. Rides include the Indian Canoe, the Rising Sun and Mountains of the Grand Canyon. Live entertainment, including shoot-outs between cowboys and Indians.
13780 Cuges-les-Pins, on the RN8 between Marseille and Toulon. Tel: 04 42 73 80 05; www.okcorral.fr. Open: Mar, Sept–Nov, Sat & Sun, 10am–5.30pm; Apr–June, Wed, Sat & Sun, 10am–5.30pm; July–Aug, daily, 10am–5.30pm. Admission charge.

Fréjus
Parc Zoologique Safari de Fréjus
You can explore this 20-hectare (49-acre) zoo on foot or by car.
Le Capitou, 83600 Fréjus. Tel: 04 98 11 37 37. Open: Nov–Feb, daily, 10.30am–4pm; Mar–May & Sept, daily, 10am–5pm; July–Aug, daily, 10am–6pm. Admission charge.

Port-Cros
Sentier Sub-marin
For keen and novice snorkellers, a do-it-yourself underwater discovery trail with information panels.
Port-Cros National Park, île de Port-Cros. Tel: 04 94 01 40 70. Open: July & Aug, daily. Admission charge.

St-Cannat
Le Village des Automates
Theme park with animated scenes and puppets: Pinocchio, Gulliver's Travels, Merlin, the circus, etc.
13760 St-Cannat, between Salon-de-Provence and Aix-en-Provence. Tel: 04 42 57 30 30; http://village.automates.free.fr. Open: Apr–Sept, daily, 10am–6pm; Oct–Mar, Wed, Sat & Sun 10am–5pm. Admission charge.

St-Tropez
Maison des Papillons
A collection of over 20,000 specimens of nocturnal butterflies and moths.
Rue Etienne Berry, St-Tropez. Tel: 04 94 97 63 45. Open: June–Aug, Wed–Mon, 10am–noon & 2–7pm; Sept–May, Wed–Mon, 10am–noon 2–6pm. Admission charge.

Sanary
Sanary-Bandol Jardin Exotique et Zoo
A pleasant zoo with a good bird collection.
Just north of exit 12 on motorway, Bandol. Tel: 04 94 29 40 38; www.zoosanary.com. Open: daily, 8am–noon & 2–7pm (till dusk in winter). Closed: Sun afternoon. Admission charge.

Septèmes-les-Vallons
Aquacity
Huge aquapark with an amazing variety of slides: free-fall shute, white-water river, cascade, water bobsleigh.
13240 Septèmes-les-Vallons, off A51 autoroute between Marseille and Aix-en-Provence. Tel: 08 26 10 12 88; www.aquacity.fr. Open: June–Sept, daily, 10am–6pm. Admission charge.

Sport and leisure

The Provençals are no different from the rest of us in their passion for *le foot* (football), motor racing, tennis, golf and watersports. What sets them apart is their love of *boules*, cycling and bullfighting. Any gravelly patch of land is likely to be commandeered as a *boules* pitch for a game that seems like an impromptu version of bowls. Nowhere near as incomprehensible as cricket or American football, it is a restful game to watch, drink in hand, from the comfort of a pavement café.

Practising for the *corrida* (bullfight) in Arles' Arènes (amphitheatre)

Cycling is a serious, and strenuous, business in Provence. The steeper the hill, the greater the challenge – and that is quite apart from the heat. The classic cycle climb is the ascent of Mont Ventoux (a regular leg of the **Tour de France**), an energy-sapping grind of around 20km (12 miles) to an altitude of nearly 2,000m (6,562ft). The Provençal predilection for bullfighting is concentrated in the south, around the Camargue. Animal-lovers can at least rejoice in the fact the bull survives in the Provençal version.

Bullfighting

Bulls come off rather better in Provence than in Spain. The usual spectacle involves the bullfighter, or *razeteurs*, in unfixing a cockade attached to the bull's horns without hurting the animal. But before you attend a bullfight, make sure that it is not the Spanish-style *mise-à-mort* encounter.

The *arènes* (Roman amphitheatres) at Arles and Nîmes are leading venues for bullfighting (*Arles tel: 08 91 70 03 70;* *www.arenes-arles.com; Nîmes tel: 08 91 70 14 01; www.arenesdenimes.com*).

Cycling

Not all of Provence is for macho, masochistic cyclists. Bring your own bicycle, or hire one locally, and enjoy the flattish lands along the Rhône Valley or the Camargue. Along the coast in summer, the sheer volume of traffic can make cycling unpleasant, though you'll at least have the last laugh when it comes to parking.

Golf

The Fédération Française de Golf regulates the sport in France. It has become very popular in the last few years and many new courses, especially on the Côte d'Azur, have opened their doors to members and guests.

Cannes Mougins Golf Club
Mougins. Tel: 08 70 12 25 050.
Fédération Française de Golf
68 rue Anatole France, 9230 Levallois-

Perret. *Tel: 01 41 49 77 00;*
www.ffg.org

Golf des Baux-de-Provence
Domaine de Mauville, Les Baux-de-Provence. Tel: 04 90 54 40 20. Email: golfbauxdeprovence@wanadoo.fr

Golfe de Cap Estérel
11km (7 miles) east of St-Raphaël. Tel: 04 94 82 55 00.

Golf de Châteaublanc (Avignon)
Morières-lès-Avignon. Tel: 04 90 33 39 08; www.golfchateaublanc.com

Golf de Digne-les-Bains
Tel: 04 92 30 58 00; www.golfdigne.com

Golf de Roquebrune (near Fréjus)
Roquebrune-St-Argens. Tel: 04 94 19 60 35; www.le-roc.fr

Golfe de Valescure
10km (6 miles) east of Fréjus. Tel: 04 94 82 40 46. Email: golfdevalescure@wanadoo.fr

Motor racing

Monaco is the spiritual home of **Formula One Grand Prix** racing. Although the narrow street circuit is totally unsuited to today's racing cars (overtaking is virtually impossible), the Grand Prix, held in May, is still the race of the season.

During Grand Prix weekend, the cars are not the only things to change gear. Prices in Monaco, never modest at the best of times, shift up another cog in response to the glamour-seeking jet setters and the captive audience of genuine fans.

The South of France's other main motor racing venue is the **Circuit Paul Ricard**. *Route des Hauts du Camp, Le Castellet, 83330 Le Beausset. Tel: 04 94 98 36 66; www.circuitpaulricard.com*

Horseriding

Horseriding and trekking are widely available in certain parts of Provence. The Camargue, in particular, has many riding centres, which offer anything from a few hours in the saddle to a full day's trekking. All equestrian activities in relation to tourism in France come under the umbrella of the centralised **Comité National du Tourisme Équestre de la Fédération Française d'Équitation**. More than 1,200 equestrian centres are listed by FFE. *9 boulevard Macdonald, 75019 Paris. Tel: 01 53 26 15 50; www.ffe.com*

Skiing

Inhabitants of the Côte d'Azur live in privileged surroundings. In winter it is quite possible to water-ski along a sunny seashore in the morning and ski on snow in the afternoon. Three major ski resorts lie within a few hours' drive of Nice: **Auron**, **Isola 2000** and **Valberg**. Despite their southern latitude, they boast excellent snow records.

A little further north, in the Alpes-de-Haute-Provence, the two major ski resorts are **Pra-Loup** and **Super-Sauze** near Barcelonnette.

Auron
Range: 1,600m–2,500m (5,250–8,200ft) with 120km (75 miles) of piste. *Office de Tourisme, 06660 St-Étienne-de-Tinée. Tel: 04 93 02 41 96.*

Isola 2000
Range: 1,800m–2,600m (5,900–8,530ft) with 112km (70 miles) of piste. *Office de Tourisme, 06420 Isola. Tel: 04 93 23 15 15.*

Pra-Loup
Range: 1,500m–2,500m (4,920–8,200ft)
160km (99 miles) of piste.
*Office de Tourisme, Maison de Pra-Loup,
04400 Pra-Loup. Tel: 04 92 84 10 04;
www.praloup.com*

Super-Sauze
Range: 1,400m–2,400m (4,590–7,875ft)
with pistes to suit all skiing abilities.
*Office de Tourisme, Immeuble Le Perce-
Neige, 04400 Le Sauze/Super-Sauze.
Tel: 04 92 81 05 61; www.sauze.com*

Valberg
Range: 1,600m–2,450m (5,250–8,040ft)
with 80km (50 miles) of piste and 50km
(31 miles) of cross-country ski trails.
*Office de Tourisme, 06470 Valberg.
Tel: 04 93 23 24 25.*

There are a number of other, smaller ski
resorts and stations in Provence,
including:
L'Audibergue, Beuil-les-Launes, Le
Boréon, La Colmiane-Valdeblore,
Esteng-d'Entraunes, Jausiers-la-Frache,
La Foux-d'Allos, La Gordoloasque-
Belvédère, Gréolières-Les-Neiges,
Montagne de Lure, Mont Ventoux,
Peira-Cava, Roubion-les-Buisses, St-
Auban, St-Dalmas-le-Selvage,
Ste-Anne-la-Condamine, St-Jean-
Montclar, Tende-Caramagne, Turini-
Camp-d'Argent and Val-Pelens-St-
Martin-d'Entraunes.

A selection of 01891 snow
information telephone numbers
operates within the UK. Some of the
resorts mentioned here are part of the
Ski France service. For further
information, contact:
*9 rue de Madrid, 75008 Paris. Tel: 04 47
42 23 32; www.skifrance.fr*

Walking and climbing
Walking and hiking are extremely well-
organised in France. A network of long-
distance footpaths and trails covers the
whole of the country, from north to
south, east to west. These marked paths
are known as 'GRs' (Sentiers des
Grandes Randonnées), each of which
bears an identifying number like a road
or motorway.

Some of the most popular walking
areas in Provence are the Luberon
Hills, Massif des Maures and Mont
Ventoux. These areas offer hilly terrain
and – in the case of the Maures and
Ventoux – a good covering of cool,
green forest.

The mountains of the Alpes-de-Haute-
Provence and Alpes-Maritimes provide a
much more serious challenge. Walkers
can spend days and weeks in this
dramatic landscape – the higher parts of
which remain snow-covered throughout
the year – stopping overnight in remote
hostels or mountain huts.

Rock climbing is a major activity in
the mountains. All levels of difficulty
can be tackled. Experienced climbers
are particularly attracted to the **Parc
National du Mercantour** (*see pp137–8*),
where the ascents range from difficult
to very difficult.

June to October is the best time to
enjoy the high mountains. Keep a
watch out for the weather – it can
change very quickly. And always be well
prepared.

Walking information
Nature & Tourisme
*rue Voltaire, 75011 Paris.
Tel: 01 43 72 15 69.*

Fédération Française de la Randonnées Pédestres
Centre d'Information, 14 rue Riquet, 75019 Paris. Tel: 01 44 89 93 93; www.ffrp.asso.fr

Climbing Information
Club Alpin Français
24 avenue Laumière, 75019 Paris. Tel: 01 53 72 87 00; www.ffcam.fr
Fédération Française de la Montagne et de l'Escalade
8 quai Marne, 75019 Paris. Tel: 01 40 18 75 59; www.ffme.fr

Watersports
Although conditions in the placid Mediterranean are not perfect for serious sailing and windsurfing, this does not seem to put many people off. There are marinas and harbours packed with expensive yachts all along the coast. Windsurfers can easily hire equipment at many of the local beaches and sports shops.

Diving conditions are good, though marine life has suffered along the Riviera through overfishing and pollution. Away from the coast, Provence's lakes and rivers provide excellent watersports opportunities.

Further information is available from the following national organisations:
Canoeing/Rafting
Fédération Française de Canoë-Kayak
87 quai de la Marne, 94340 Joinville-le-Pont. Tel: 01 45 11 08 50; www.ffck.fr

Diving
Fédération Française d'Études et des Sports Sous-Marins
24 quai de Rive-Neuve, 13284 Marseille. Tel: 04 91 33 99 31; www.ffessm.fr

Water-skiing
Fédération Française de Ski Nautique
27 rue Athènes, 75009 Paris. Tel: 01 53 20 19 19; www.ffsa.fr

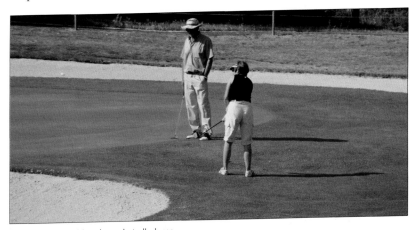

Golfing opportunities abound at all places

The black cypress and the silvery olive tree dominate large parts of the Provençal landscape. The mournful beauty of the cypress has inspired many a poet; the olive, a tough evergreen, serves a more practical purpose. Originally imported from Greece, it has long had a vital role in the agrarian economy of Provence.

The hardy olive

One of the principal virtues of the olive, for the canny farmers of Provence, is that it thrives in barren areas, taking root in poor, rocky soil and surviving great heat and aridity. What is more, it is long-lived: many of the groves climbing the hillsides have been tended by succeeding generations of farmers. The trees grow to a height of around 7.5m (25ft) and often achieve impressive girth. Its handsome hard wood is sometimes carved into kitchen utensils and other objects.

As anyone who has visited a Provençal market will confirm, olives are taken very seriously in this part of France. For a start, there are stalls dedicated to the sale of olives and nothing else; and you are not – heaven forbid! – given a choice of merely black or green, but myriad variations on a theme, all laid out in open containers for tasting beforehand. There are olives with garlic, olives with peppers and olives with herbs, bitter and smooth-tasting olives – even plain black and green olives.

Oil and cosmetics

Then there are the bottles of olive

oil, a staple ingredient of Provençal culinary art. The extraction of oil from the ripened fruit is a comparatively simple process, and over the years the oil press has been as widely used in Provence as the wine press.

The olives, black when ripe, are first pressed to a pasty consistency, then put in woollen bags and subjected to considerable pressure. The resulting product is considered the finest of vegetable oils, and is used not only in food preparation but in fine soaps and cosmetics.

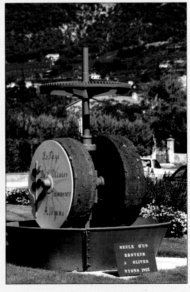

Nyons is a well-known centre of olive production where visitors can see the entire process from growing to processing, and then buy the many varieties of the fruit

Food and drink

Provence, like the rest of France, reveres its food. Meals are anything but a means to an end. They rise above mere sustenance into occasions with aesthetic and social dimensions – which explains why meals are never hurried, there are deliberate pauses between courses, and everything still stops for lunch.

Olive oils and fancy vinegars

You will always find exceptions to these generalisations, but they will be confined to the larger towns and cities where the universal fast-food mentality is making its presence felt. In small-town Provence and in the country areas, traditional values still apply. Ask the locals – they will always know the best places to eat.

Restaurants range from the very expensive (usually along the coast) to the amazingly cheap. Go for the fixed-price menu of three or four courses, with limited choice per course. Many restaurants offer a few versions of these, ranging from the basic *menu touristique* (which usually features chicken, trout, steak and chips, etc) to the elaborate *menu gastronomique* with regional specialities.

Bread (a cut-up *baguette*) is always provided, along with water. House wine is usually quite inexpensive, though some of the classier bottles can be surprisingly dear in comparison to their supermarket price. For those with a small appetite, many cafés and bars serve snacks and light meals. Cafés will also serve breakfast – a large cup of milky coffee, bread, jam and sometimes croissants.

There are few vegetarians in France, and French restaurateurs in general do not see any need to make special allowances on their menus for customers on a strict meat- and fish-free diet. There are, however, vegetarian restaurants in Marseille (several), Nice and Aix-en-Provence. Everywhere else, the best options are either to choose a salad from the menu and be prepared to pick out any meat or fish in it, or to look for a foreign-run restaurant where the owners are more likely to understand vegetarian requirements.

Along with wine, the staple drink of Provence is *pastis*, a strong aniseed-flavoured aperitif served with ice and water (*see pp170–71*). Locals swear that they can tell the difference between the main brands, Pernod, Ricard and Pastis. Beer is served by the bottle or, in most cafés, on draught as *bière pression*, the cheaper option.

Soft drinks include *orange pressé* (freshly squeezed orange juice), *citron* (lemon) *pressé*, and fizzy Orangina. There is a wide choice of mineral waters including the famous Perrier, which is bottled locally in the west of the Rhône delta. Only ask for *café* if you like your coffee served black at paint-stripping strength. Most visitors prefer the *café crème* or *café au lait* version served with milk.

Prices

The listing that follows is a selection of places to eat across a wide price range. The following star ratings used to indicate the average cost per person of a three-course meal, not including drink. All taxes and service charges are usually included in the price.

★   less than €30
★★   €31–46
★★★   €47–76
★★★★   more than €77

Where to eat
Agay
Côté Jardin ★★
Wonderful garden setting for this surprisingly good small restaurant.
Rue du 11 novembre.
Tel: 04 94 82 79 98.

Aix-en-Provence
Au Basilic
Gourmand ★/★★
Excellent cuisine at affordable prices.
6 rue du Griffon.
Tel: 04 42 96 08 58.

L'Amphitryon ★/★★
A delightful historic setting. Good regional dishes and fair prices.
2–4 rue Paul Doumer.
Tel: 04 42 26 54 10.

Le Clos de la Violette ★★★★
One of the top restaurants in Aix, which serves innovative and traditional cuisine. For best value, eat here at lunchtime on weekdays.
10 rue de la Violette.
Tel: 04 42 23 30 71.

Antibes
La Toscana ★★
A restaurant-brasserie offering Italian cuisine and French dishes such as fondue bourgignonue.
Quartier de la Brague – the N7 coast road just over 4km (2¹/₂ miles) from Antibes.
Tel: 04 93 33 36 65;
www.toscana.resto.com
Le Relais du Postillon ★★
Former staging post, with great ambience and traditional Provençal fare.
8 rue du Championet.
Tel: 04 93 34 20 77.
Restaurant de Bacon ★★★★
Apart from Marseille, this is the best place to savour *bouillabaisse*, the traditional fish stew from Provence. Also try one of the many other delicious seafood dishes on offer. There is also a panoramic view of the bay.
Boulevard de Bacon, Cap d'Antibes.
Tel: 04 93 61 50 02;
www. restaurantdebacon.com

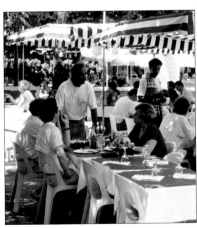

Antibes has a wide range of eating places to choose from

Arles

L'Atelier de Jean-Luc Rabanel ★★★

Located in the historic centre, this restaurant serves food cooked with organic ingredients only and also offers cookery classes.
7 rue des Carmes.
Tel: 04 90 91 07 69;
www.rabanel.com

Brasserie Nord Pinus ★★/★★★

Part of the Nord Pinus hotel, one-time home-from-home to artists such as Picasso and Cocteau, this old-world brasserie still pulls in the crowds for its excellent and often innovative cuisine.
Place Forum.
Tel: 04 90 93 44 44.

Ferme Auberge de Barbegal ★★

A lovely farm outside Arles offering accommodation, and meals using only their own products.
Domaine du Grand Barbegal, Périphéric Est d'Arles. Tel: 04 90 54 63 69;
www.barbegal.com

Jardin de Manon ★★

Just a short walk from the Roman centre, this excellent-value restaurant offers good Provençal dishes with flair.
14 avenue Alyscamps.
Tel: 04 90 93 38 68.

Avignon

Christian Étienne ★★★★

An elegant restaurant and refined cuisine to match. One of Provence's famed temples of gastronomy.
10 rue Mons.
Tel: 04 90 86 16 50.

La Fourchette ★★

A perennially good-value bistro with local specialities.
17 rue Racine.
Tel: 04 90 85 20 93.

Hiely-Lucullus ★★★★

A charming restaurant with a formidable reputation. One of Provence's gastronomic shrines.
5 rue de la République.
Tel: 04 90 86 17 07.

Les Baux-de-Provence

Auberge de la Benbengudo ★★★★

A delightful *bastide* with lovely rooms and a good restaurant. Worth the short journey out of Les Baux.
Vallon de l'Arcoule, route d'Arles.
Tel: 04 90 54 32 54.

L'Oustau de Baumanière ★★★★

Another picturesque country house turned hotel and restaurant. Home grown produce and a fine chef nurture a refined cuisine which is truly unique and memorable. Treat yourself but expect to pay a big bill – it is way off the humble price scale.
Val d'Enfer.
Tel: 04 90 54 33 07.

Cairanne

Auberge Castel Miréio ★/★★

An elegantly appointed restaurant in a small hotel in the heart of Côtes-du-Rhône wine country. Good service and food.
Route d'Orange.
Tel: 04 90 30 82 20.

Cannes

La Farigoule ★★

Authentic Provençal cuisine at reasonable prices.
78 boulevard Carnot.
Tel: 04 93 39 22 23.

Le Fouquet's Cannes ★★

A popular brasserie with terrace, specialising in traditional Provençal fare.
10 boulevard de la Croisette.
Tel: 04 92 98 77 05.

La Frégate ★/★★

A popular pizzeria for those who tire of fish dishes.
26 boulevard Jean Hibert.
Tel: 04 93 39 45 39.

La Mère Besson ★★★★

A favourite Cannes restaurant serving

authentically prepared traditional specialities.
13 rue des Freres-Pradignac.
Tel: 04 93 39 59 24.

Cassis
Il Ristorante ★
Pizzeria-trattoria specialising in pasta and Italian cuisine.
Quai des Baux.
Tel: 04 42 01 35 19.
Jardin d'Émile ★★/★★★
Attractive small hotel with good restaurant, overlooking the Calanque of Port-Miou, just 1km (²/₃ mile) from Cassis. Pretty ambience and good cuisine.
23 avenue Gauteaume.
Tel: 04 42 01 80 55.

Fayence
Temps des Cerises ★★/★★★
In a traditional house with a delightful terrace area, innovative cuisine.
Place de Ia République.
Tel: 04 94 76 01 19.

Fréjus
Les Bories ★★★/★★★★
Wonderful position for this good restaurant. New Provençal cuisine and a fine wine cellar.
Route de l'Abbaye de Senanque.
Tel: 04 90 72 00 51.
Les Potiers ★★
A small, convivial restaurant in the centre of town.
135 rue des Potiers.
Tel: 04 94 51 33 74.

Lunching *al fresco* at a busy marketplace

Gordes
La Mayanelle ★★★/★★★★
An up-market restaurant serving Provençal fare with flair.
6 rue Combe.
Tel: 04 90 72 00 28.

Marseille
Une Table, au Sud ★★★
A restaurant to note and a star chef who provides the best Provençal fare.
Off the port area.
2 quai du Port.
Tel: 04 91 90 63 53.

Monaco
Le Café de Paris ★★/★★★★
You do not have to spend a fortune here to enjoy a reasonable meal. International dishes are served in glittering *belle époque*-style surroundings.
Place du Casino,
Monte Carlo.
Tel: (377) 92 16 20 20.
Le Louis XV ★★★★
The most elegant – and still one of the best – restaurants in Monaco, located in the equally renowned Hotel de Paris. Outstanding cuisine served in a formal atmosphere. Very expensive, but, considering that you might well find yourself seated next to royalty, worth it.

Place du Casino.
Tel: (377) 92 16 30 01.

Mougins
Le Feu Follet ★★/★★★
In a town known for expensive fine dining, this restaurant offers quality cuisine at affordable rates.
Place de la Maire.
Tel: 04 93 90 15 78.

Nice
L'Ane Rouge ★★★★
Small, but with a huge reputation as Nice's best seafood restaurant. Located on the harbour.
7 quai Deux-Emmanuel.
Tel: 04 93 89 49 63.

Nîmes
Au Flan Coco ★/★★
A good address. Small, inexpensive and has a friendly atmosphere.
31 rue Mûrier-d'Espagne.
Tel: 04 66 21 84 81.
Le Restaurant des Arenes ★★/★★★
An intimate restaurant in a vaulted room, serving traditional Provençal food.
3 rue de la République.
Tel: 04 66 76 15 14.
Zucca Magica ★/★★
Fine dining in a vegetarian restaurant? Zucca Magica breaks all those preconceptions

with its Italian-influenced cuisine. Excellent value.
4 bis quai Papacino.
Tel: 04 93 56 25 27.

Orange
Le Parvis ★★/★★★
Freshly grown local products, traditional cooking with an original touch and well-priced menus explain this restaurant's popularity.
3 cours Pourtoules.
Tel: 04 90 34 82 00.
Le Yaca ★/★★
Stylish setting for this excellent restaurant. Mediterranean-style cuisine.
24 place Sylvain.
Tel: 04 90 34 70 03.

Salon de Provence
Le Château de Richebois ★★★
Just outside Salon de Provence, this restaurant in a château is set in peaceful grounds and serves traditional regional cuisine.
Route d'Eyguières.
Tel: 04 90 56 85 85;
www.richebois.com

St-Raphaël
L'Arbousier ★★/★★★
A modern ambience and the gastronomic menu ensure the

popularity of this excellent restaurant.
4 ave de Valescure.
Tel: 04 94 95 25 00.

St-Rémy-de-Provence

Le Bistro d'Eygalières ★★★★

In a nearby village, southeast of St-Rémy, this newish restaurant has risen rapidly to renown for its outstanding cuisine. Provençal with innovative touches.
Rue de la République.
Tel: 04 90 90 60 34.

La France ★

Good-value French regional fare on fixed-price menus.
2 avenue Fauconnet.
Tel: 04 90 92 11 56.

St Tropez

Bistrot des Lices ★★★/★★★★

Glamorous bistro that pulls in the celebrities. A perennial favourite.
3 place des Lices.
Tel: 04 94 97 11 33.

La Table du Marché ★/★★★

A popular venue for its local specialities and innovative, changing menu.
38 rue Georges Clemenceau.
Tel: 04 94 97 85 20.

Lei Mouscardins ★★★★

Port-side restaurant with a good reputation for its Provençal menus. Prices are high because of location and well-heeled clientele.
Tour du Portalet.
Tel: 04 94 97 29 00

Vaison-la-Romaine

Le Beffroi ★★/★★★

The views from this 16th-century hotel and restaurant are expansive and take in all the medieval town. Good menus featuring regional cuisine.
Rue le l'Évêché, Haute Ville. Tel: 04 90 36 04 71.

Le Moulin à Huile ★★★

Gastronomic dining took a turn for the better when this restaurant gained its Michelin star. A fine position near the river matches an inventive cuisine.
1 quai du Maréchal Foch.
Tel: 04 90 36 20 67.

Eating out at Le Beffroi in Vaison-la-Romaine

Breakfast overlooking the plains of western Provence

Provençal cuisine

In classic Provençal cuisine, freshness and inherent flavour are everything. Provençals leave the rich, creamy sauces to their northern countryfolk, preferring instead to let the ingredients speak for themselves.

Although garlic is liberally used, it tends to be milder in the south of France than in the north. Garlic is a mainstay of the distinctive Provençal cuisine, along with olive oil, herbs like basil, rosemary and thyme, and the tomato, or *pomme d'amour* (love apple). If you have been brought up on the bland, shrink-wrapped supermarket version of the tomato, then fear not:

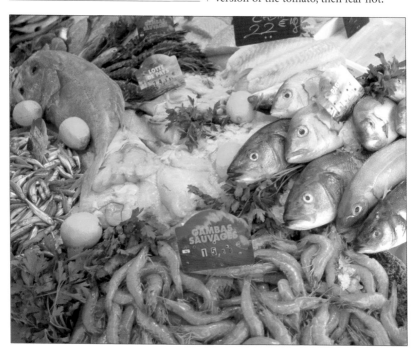

What will it be for dinner today?

the plump, tasty Provençal variety is similar only in colour.

Harvest of the sea

The Provençals are justly proud of their fish dishes such as *soupe de poisson*, a work of art taking hours to prepare. A variation on this theme is the famous *bouillabaisse*, a speciality of the Marseille coast. *Bouillabaisse* is not really a soup at all. The fish are served on a side dish, while the garlic- and saffron-flavoured stew in which they were cooked comes separately so that diners can dunk their bread into it. Another classic dish is *bourride*, a white fish stew served with *aïoli*, a rich mayonnaise of garlic and olive oil known as 'the butter of Provence'.

Meat, cheese and fruit

Lamb also figures prominently in the local cuisine. The spicy *agneau de Sisteron* comes from the mountain pastures of Provence, while the lambs grazing on the salt marshes of the coast provide *agneau de pré-salé. Boeuf à la gardianne* is a popular beef stew cooked with red wine, vegetables, black olives and herbs. Another speciality of the region is *farci* (stuffed vegetable). Onions are stuffed with garlic, cabbages with parsley and sausage.

Cheeses, which are served before the dessert, include the local *banon*, wrapped in vine or chestnut leaves, and the peppery *poivre d'âne*. Fruit is plentiful – and be sure to make the most of the mouthwatering melons, best bought in quantity from local markets when they are just beginning to split.

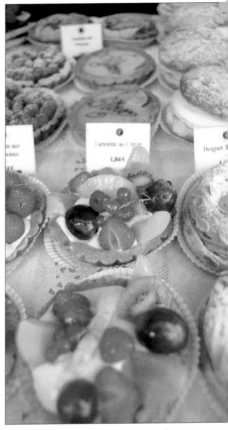

Delectable desserts are an integral part of Provençal cuisine

Eating out in Provence is a delight, and the food seems to taste even better when you dine *al fresco* on a terrace shaded by parasols or vines. Lunch is served early, from about noon, with dinner from 7–7.30pm. Fast food is an anathema to the Provençals, and so is fast service. You are meant to take your time, and each course is served to be savoured, not rushed. *Bon appétit!*

Drinking a glass or two of a chewy, deeply textured Côtes-du-Rhône Villages – a Cairanne perhaps, or a Gigondas, Rasteau or Vacqueyras – on the terrace on a warm summer's evening is one of the great pleasures of Provence. And it is a pleasure made even more satisfying in the knowledge that this full-bodied red wine, bought direct from the local vineyard, has cost little more than the standard supermarket plonk back home.

The reds of the Rhône
Parts of Provence are almost entirely dedicated to the production of wine: drive along the flanks of the Rhône Valley around Orange and Avignon, and you will see regimented rows of vines stretching into the distance. These vineyards yield the robust, peppery generic Côtes-du-Rhône and the even better versions named after individual villages or growers.

The top wine from the region is Châteauneuf-du-Pape, a full, rich red with a perfumed raspberry bouquet, which often does not peak until a decade or so after bottling.

Although its reds reign supreme (a consequence of the hot climate), Provence produces wines to suit all occasions. In addition to the deep – and highly alcoholic – reds, there are delicate rosés and dry and sweet whites. Tavel and Lirac rosés are both exceptionally good. Beaumes-de-Venise is mostly famous for its thick, sweet wine made from the muscat grape and served chilled as an apéritif or

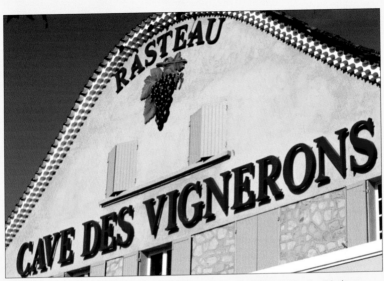

dessert wine (a similar wine is produced in Rasteau), though some exceptional red wines are also made here.

The wines from the coastal strip around Bandol – reds, rosés and whites – have a character all their own, while the whites of nearby Cassis are fresh and aromatic.

Other, less well-known wine-producing areas in Provence include Côtes-du-Ventoux, Côtes-du-Luberon, Côtes-de-Provence and Côteaux d'Aix.

Strong stuff

Pay attention to the alcoholic content of Provençal wines. It tends to be higher – in some cases, substantially so – than the usual 10 to 12 degrees. The same word of warning applies to *pastis*, the traditional aniseed-flavoured spirit drink of Provence. Normally over 50 degrees proof (though you can purchase weaker versions), it is served as a long drink, and the spirit turns milky when ice and water are added.

The region's vineyards produce some of France's most famous red wines

Hotels and accommodation

For families and couples, hotels in France usually offer good value because you pay by the room, not per person. Along the Riviera, however, this money-saving arrangement is undermined by high room rates, but in rural Provence you will usually be pleasantly surprised by the accommodation you can purchase for a relatively modest sum.

The world's most famous people have stayed here

Many visitors to Provence – especially families or large groups of friends – prefer to self-cater. Along the coast, and in the hills just inland, there is a large choice of apartments and luxury villas. Summer rates for the sought-after properties are high. For better value, go further inland – which, in any case, is the true Provence – and rent a more modest country property.

Camping, of course, is the ultimate budget alternative. The French are a nation of ardent campers, so you can expect to find an excellent choice of sites with comprehensive facilities.

For business travellers

The main commercial centres of Cannes, Marseille, Monaco and Nice have many three- and four-star hotels geared to the business traveller and conference delegate. Cannes, for example, has the Noga Hilton (*5 boulevard la Croisette; tel: 04 92 99 70 00; www.hilton.com*), while at Nice there is the Holiday Inn Nice (*20 boulevard Victor Hugo; tel: 04 97 03 22 22; www.holiday-inn.fr*). All major hotel

chains have interactive websites in various languages. It is usually more informative and sometimes easier to search these rather than to telephone. Listed below are some of the UK toll-reduced telephone numbers and websites for the larger business hotel chains in France.
Concorde Hotels *Tel: 0800 0289 880; www.concorde-hotels.com*
Hilton International *Tel: 0800 7741 500; www.hilton.com*
Holiday Inn *Tel: 0800 911 617; www.ichotelsgroup.com*
Best Western *Tel: 0800 393 130; www.bestwestern.co.uk*
Le Meridién, Novotel and Mercure
Tel: 0825 012 011 (Novotel), 0825 883 333 (Mercure), 0800 402 215 (Le Meridién); www.lemeridien.com, www.novotel.com, www.mercure.com
Ibis *Tel: 0892 686 686; www.ibishotel.com*
Sofitel *Tel: 0825 012 011; www.accor-hotels.com*

Hotels

Hotels in France are classified by the Ministry of Tourism as follows:

Four Star L = luxury
Four Star = deluxe
Three Star = first class
Two Star = tourist class, good quality
One Star = budget.
For overnight accommodation you
usually pay by the room (based on a
twin/double), and breakfast is extra. You
can get a bed in a *gite d'etape* for €8,
although the cheapest hotel rooms are
usually upwards of €25. For a modestly
good hotel expect to pay €70–100, and
really nice hotels start at €100. A suite in
a very good hotel will set you back €300
or more. Prices are cheaper inland.

Provençal hotels

Provence's romantic image of sun-kissed
stone farmhouses and elegant country
residences is a reality. More and more
small hotels (from 4–20 rooms but not
usually at the budget end of the price
spectrum) are opening their doors as
tasteful renovation plans are finished,
and welcome visitors in search of their
Provençal dream. These hotels are rarely
affiliated with groups (they are too
small) and recommendations are passed
by word of mouth by those in the know.
However, most have websites, and a
good search on the web will inevitably
yield many delightful and non-
commercial properties.

Hotel chains

France has many hotel groups and
associations. The largest cover the entire
country, though some are confined to a
particular region. The accommodation
ranges from purpose-built places (such
as Formule 1 or Campanile) to
beautifully converted country properties,

historic castles or elegant townhouses
rich in atmosphere and charm.

Châteaux et Hôtels de France

There is a good selection of these
characterful hotels around the Rhône
Valley and along the coast between
St-Tropez and Nice.
*Tel: 08 92 23 00 75; from abroad +33 172
729 202.*
In UK: *tel: 020 7616 0300;
www.chateauxhotels.com*

Logis de France

With over 3,000 hotels-restaurants
throughout the country, from small and
comfortable, to extremely comfortable,
the Logis are individually owned hotels
recognisable by their yellow and green
logo. They offer good hospitality and
service and bring their clients regional
cuisine. Contact:
**Fédération Nationale des Logis de
France**
*83 ave d'Italie, 75013 Paris; tel: 01 45 84
70 00, fax: 01 45 83 59 66.*
Reservations: tel: 01 45 84 83 84.
In UK: *tel: 0870 240 5903; www.logis-de-
france.fr or www.allofrance.co.uk*

The lap of luxury
Some of the stylish hotels in the South of
France are favoured by the expense-is-no-
object business traveller – and anyone else
who can afford the glamorous life. Two such
places are the famous **Carlton Inter-
Continental** in Cannes (*58 La Croisette;
tel: 04 93 06 40 06; www.canneshotels.
intercontinental.com*) and the equally
celebrated **Negresco** in Nice (*37 promenade
des Anglais; tel: 04 93 16 64 00; fax: 04 93
88 35 68*). In Monaco the last word in luxury
is offered by the **Paris** (*place du Casino; tel:
(377) 98 06 30 00; fax: (377) 98 06 59 13*).

Campanile

Similar to the Climat de France, Première Class and Kyriad groups of hotels (all owned by Envergure), Campanile offers modern, purpose-built two-star hotels with restaurants. Their website is geared to answer all questions – and to make bookings irrespective of language.
Tel: 08 25 00 30 03; from abroad: 33 1 6462 4646; www.envergure.fr

Formule 1

Inexpensive, purpose-built hotels, part of the huge Accor group, Formule 1 hotels are usually located on the periphery of towns and are, for driving tourists, a great standby. For more information:
www.hotelformule1.com, www.accorhotels.com

Relais et Châteaux

Top of the range, and noted for their comfort, location and often excellent restaurants, these individually owned properties are usually beautifully converted historic buildings.
33 boulevard Malesherbes, 75008 Paris. Tel: 08 25 32 32 32, fax: 01 40 06 04 35; www.relaischateaux.com

Le Relais du Silence

An unusual group of privately owned hotels that aim to offer tranquillity in a fine location. Often boasting good restaurants.
Tel: 01 44 49 90 00; www.silencehotel.com

Bed and breakfast

The nearest equivalent to the British B&B is the **Gîtes-Chambres d'Hôtes**, usually situated in farmhouses or villages and ranging in size from one to several bedrooms.
La Maison des Gîtes de France, 59 rue Saint-Lazare, 75439 Paris Cedex 09. Tel: 01 49 70 75 75; www.gites-de-france.fr

Self-catering

The **Gîtes Rural de France** are holiday homes, usually in country or village locations, that offer accommodation across four different grades. Although they have a rustic image, some *gîtes* – especially those in the top categories – can provide comfortable and charming accommodation, and might even have a private swimming pool. In Provence, *gîtes* are in great demand, so if you want the peak summer months, book early (*see above for address details*).

There are many companies that specialise in letting private houses and villas. Ask your travel agent for details, or look out for the newspaper adverts.

Camping

Campsites range from the deliberately basic in the hills and mountains – for those who want to savour the natural environment – to the big family complexes inland and along the coast with swimming pools, restaurants and central facilities. The French are passionate – and extremely professional – campers, so you can expect the big sites to have the full range of amenities, including swimming pools, shops and family recreation facilities. Some also have permanently sited, fully furnished mobile homes for six to eight people; travel agents can advise you of firms that specialise in mobile homes, as well as large pre-erected furnished tents, on quality campsites.

At the other end of the scale there are simple sites – usually in rural locations – with basic facilities. The best overnight rates are to be found at municipal campsites (camping municipal) run by local authorities. Camping *à la ferme* (on the farm) is also good value for money. Expect to pay hefty premiums for camping along the Côte d'Azur. For full details on campsites, contact the **French Tourist Office's Maison de la France** (*178 Piccadilly, London W1V 0AL; tel: 09068 244123; http://uk.franceguide.com*). Also informative are the sites: *www.holidayfrance.org.uk, www.allezfrance.com, www.allofrance.co.uk*

Fédération Française de Camping et de Caravanning

78 rue de Rivoli, 75004 Paris. Tel: 01 42 72 84 08; www.ffcc.fr

Youth accommodation

Auberges de Jeunesse (Youth Hostels) are a good budget option, particularly for single travellers (if you are travelling as a couple or in groups, cheap hotels – where you pay by the room – will usually be just as good value). To take advantage of hostel accommodation, join the International Youth Hostel Federation through YHA, *2nd Floor, Gate House, Fretherne Road, Welwyn Garden City, Herts AL8 6RD. Tel: 01707 324170; www.hihostels.com*. You can also join at most French hostels. If you want a little more luxury, then try the **Foyers**

des Jeunes Travailleurs (*www.ufjt.org*). Available in some of the larger towns, these hostels provide comfortable, low-priced accommodation for students and young workers.

How to book

Contact the French Government Tourist Office (*see p188*). The office in your country may well produce specialist books on *gîtes*, for example. You will also find it worthwhile to contact direct the *département(s)* of Provence in which you are interested (*see p188*). They should be able to send you detailed lists of hotels, *gîtes*, campsites, etc, for their area.

Outside the Hotel Forum at Arles

On business

Coastal Provence is nowadays as much a business destination as a place for holidays and leisure. Indeed, the balance has swung in favour of the business traveller in places like Nice and Cannes, which now rely more on conventions, exhibitions and meetings than on their pleasure-seeking clientele of old.

Nice airport is a regional hub for business travellers

Business delegates are big spenders; on average, their daily expenditure amounts to anything between €200 and €350 per person. The French Business Travel Club (Club Français du Tourisme d'Affaires Réceptif, or CFTAR) has been established to service and encourage this trade. This government-approved organisation brings together more than 120 members representing all facets of business travel – convention facilities, accommodation, ground handling, study tours, seminars, transportation, etc. For further information, contact the French Government Tourist Office in your country (*see* Tourist Offices *for address details, p188*).

The big three

Cannes, Monaco and Nice are the three destinations that attract most of the Côte d'Azur's business and conference trade. All three have major modern convention centres in imposing – and stunning – locations that reflect their pre-eminence within the local economy.

CANNES

Palais des Festivals et des Congrès (Cannes Conference Centre)
A vast modern building overlooking the harbour, with adaptable floor space and full back-up of the latest technology.
La Croisette, 06403 Cannes.
Tel: 04 93 39 01 01;
www.palaisdesfestivals.com
Also contact: **Connect-Events**
Conference organiser, product launches.
68 rue d'Antibes, 06400 Cannes.
Tel: 04 93 99 99 39, fax: 04 97 06 54 42;
www.connectevents.com

MONACO

Rainier III Auditorium (Monte Carlo Convention Centre and Auditorium)
This is part of a boldly designed complex of buildings fronting the sea below the casino.
Boulevard Louis II, Monte Carlo, 98030 Monaco. Tel: (377) 93 10 84 00.
Centre de Rencontres Internationales (International Conference Centre)
Above the harbour; it complements the Centre de Congrès Auditorium.
12 avenue d'Ostende, Monte Carlo.
Tel: (377) 93 10 86 00.

Further enquiries concerning business and conference matters (including more details on the above centres) should be addressed to the following offices.

In Monaco
Direction du Tourisme et des Congrès de la Principauté de Monaco
2a boulevard des Moulins, Monte Carlo, MC 98030 Monaco Cedex. Tel: (377) 92 16 61 66; www.monaco-congres.com

In UK
Monaco Government Tourist and Convention Office
2nd Floor, 205 Harbour Yard, Chelsea Harbour, London SW10 0XF. Tel: 020 7352 9962, fax: 020 7352 2103.

In USA
Monaco Government Tourist and Convention Bureau Offices
565 Fifth Avenue, 23rd floor, New York, NY 10017. Tel: (212) 286 3330, fax: (212) 286 9890; www.monaco-tourism.com

NICE
Acropolis (Nice Conference Centre)
The ultimate in business communications and support facilities, it is set in magnificent gardens decorated with sculptures by famous artists.
1 esplanade Kennedy, 06302 Nice Cedex 4. Tel: 04 93 92 83 51, fax: 04 93 92 83 48; www.nice-acropolis.com
Hotel Palais de la Méditerranée
In the centre of Nice, this hotel has a business centre.
www.lepalaisdelamediterranee.com

You can also find information from Nice's Chamber of Commerce at *www.businessriviera.com*

Flying in
The success of the Riviera as a business and conference centre is largely due to the existence of Nice-Côte d'Azur International Airport, only 8km (5 miles) from the centre of Nice. Terminal 1 is for international and domestic flights; Terminal 2 is for domestic flights only.

In the arrivals area you will find the 2A Services (short for Accueil Affaires Services), which is run by the Chamber of Commerce and Industry. It provides multilingual hostesses who can arrange whatever you need to carry out your business.
Centre d'Affaires de l'Aeroport de Nice. Tel: 04 93 21 30 73; www.niceaeroport.fr

Further information
The Economist Intelligence Unit publishes quarterly reports on France, as well as a regular country profile, which contain essential business information.
Economist Intelligence Unit, Publications Department
25 St James's Street, London SW1A 1HG. Tel: 020 7830 7000.

The Department of Trade and Industry (DTI) also publishes a country profile on France and may be able to assist with market research costs (up to 50 per cent) if you intend doing business in France. It organises the representation of British firms at trade fairs in Nice and elsewhere.
Department of Trade and Industry, Business in Europe Branch
1 Victoria Street, London SW1H 0ET. Tel: 020 7215 5000; www.dti.gov.org/publications
Also contact:
French Chamber of Commerce
21 Dartmouth St, Westminster, London SW1H 9BP. Tel: 020 7304 4040; fax: 020 7304 7034; www.ccfgb.co.uk

P r a c t i c a l   g u i d e

Arriving
By car

With the ease of access to the Continent and the excellent motorway system in France, many visitors choose to drive to Provence or the Côte d'Azur. The most popular cross-Channel Route is now Le Shuttle, the Eurotunnel (*tel. 0870 535 3535; www.eurotunnel.com*) train route leaving from near Folkestone to Calais/Coquelles with up to four departures per hour during peak times and a crossing time of just 35 minutes. Alternatively, the ferries from Dover to Calais (P&O, UK *tel: 0870 598 0333;* France *08 25 12 01 56; www.POferries.com* and Seafrance, *tel: 08704 431 653; www.seafrance.com*) are a more leisurely (and, on a good day, more scenic) way to cross the Channel. For a longer crossing, the ferry services run from Portsmouth to St-Malo, Cherbourg, Caen and Le Havre (contact Brittany Ferries, *tel: 0870 366 9765; www.brittany-ferries.com* or P&O for details of their crossings); and from Newhaven to Dieppe (contact P&O for details of their crossings).

Visitors who want to travel by train with their car can board at Calais and alight in Avignon or Nice (for information, contact Motorail bookings, *tel: 0870 241 5415; www.frenchmotorail. com* and Rail Savers, *tel: 0870 750 7070; www.railsavers.com*).

From Calais, there is the autoroute (motorway), all the way to the south of France (Calais to Nice is around 1,220km (758 miles), depending on your route, and takes around 11 hours

to drive). It is the fastest way to arrive in the south of the country, and although the tolls are quite expensive, and the route often congested at holiday times (avoid at all cost Saturday travel in peak season), it is still the best option.

The easiest route from Calais is to avoid the congestion of Paris' *périphérique* ring road, and to take the A26/A5/A31 route, rejoining the A6 north of Dijon.

If you prefer to drive at a more leisurely pace, taking a few days to reach Provence, then use the excellent toll-free system of well-maintained and marked N (national) and D (departmental) roads. As you pass through towns, villages and beautiful countryside on these less travelled routes, you will get a real taste of the country as a whole, and the changing character of the land as you journey southwards. There are numerous *gîtes* and hotels (*see pp172–4*) along the way. A useful site for gauging driving conditions is *www.bison-fute.equipement.gov.fr*

By train

Rail passengers without a car will find that the SNCF's (*www.sncf.fr*) excellent TGV (Train à Grande Vitesse) services are the fastest way to reach Avignon, Marseille, St-Raphaël or Nice. If combining this with a ticket on the Eurostar (*www.eurostar.com*) from London (Waterloo), a change in train will be necessary either in Paris or Lille. For travel on the intercity (Grandes Lignes) or regional (TER) trains, a range of tickets and rail passes at advantageous tariffs can be bought through the Rail

Shop (Rail Europe Travel Centre, 178
Piccadilly, London W1J 9AL; *tel: 08702
414 243; www.raileurope.co.uk*).

By coach
National Express Eurolines are a budget
alternative to rail travel. Coaches operate
direct on a number of routes including
six weekly summer schedule services to
Avignon and Nîmes, while destinations
on the Côte d'Azur are served three
times a week with a change of coach in
Lyons. For full details contact: National
Express (*tel: 08705 808 080;
www.nationalexpress.com*).

By air
Provence and the Côte d'Azur are well
served by scheduled flights to a number
of airports: Nice-Côte d'Azur (*tel: 08 20
42 33 33*), Marseille-Provence (*tel: 04 42
14 14 14*) and Nîmes-Arles-Camargue
(*tel: 04 66 70 49 49*). Lyon-St-Exupery
(*tel: 08 26 80 08 26*) is also worth
considering, since the rapid autoroute
links from Lyons to the rest of the
region make it a convenient gateway for
the northern parts of Provence.

Airlines serving these airports include:
British Airways
(*www.britishairways.com*).
Air France (*www.airfrance.com*).
Ryanair (*www.ryanair.com*).
EasyJet (*www.easyjet.com*).
British Midland (*www.flybmi.com*, or
www.bmibaby.com).

Camping
See pp174–5.

Children
See pp154–5.

Climate
Provence, which consists of high
mountains as well as a Mediterranean
coastline, has some regional variations
in its climate; for example, the ferocious
wind known as the *mistral* (*see p6*)
affects mainly the Rhône Valley.
Nevertheless, it is safe to say that,
overall, Provence is a sunny place. Along
the Côte d'Azur there are 2,500–2,800
hours of sunshine per year.

June and September are the best
months to travel. The weather is
pleasantly hot (and can remain so into
October), the days are long, and there
are no summer crowds. It can become
very hot in July and August, especially
away from sea breezes.

It does not rain very often in Provence
– but when it does, it pours. Late August
can bring tremendous thunderstorms
and torrential downpours. Average
rainfall, though, is low, less than 800mm

MARSEILLE

Weather Conversion Chart
25.4mm = 1 inch
°F = 1.8 x °C + 32

a year. If Provence has a rainy season, then it is in November and December.

Conversion tables

Clothes except for women's dresses, and shoes sizes follow the standard sizes for the Rest of Europe. *See tables opposite.*

Crime

Provence is not immune to the growing problem of car theft. It is particularly rife in the Camargue and some of the main cities. So be careful where you park your car, and make sure that all valuables are locked away safely out of sight. Similarly, try not to stand out in a crowd – tourists are perceived as soft targets by thieves.

Wear a moneybelt, or keep your bag strapped across your body. If you are robbed, contact the police immediately and get a signed note for your insurance claim (*déclaration de perte*).
See also Emergency Telephone Numbers.

Customs regulations

Those allowed to enter France without a visa (for stays of up to 90 days) include citizens from EU countries, the USA, Canada and New Zealand. All categories of travellers, except holders of a National Identity Card, must be in possession of a valid passport. For full details, please check with the nearest French Consulate.

Travellers from South Africa will need a visa. People requiring visas should get them in their country of residence, as it may prove difficult to get them elsewhere. For further visa information check:
www.diplomatie.gouv.fr/venir/visas

Driving

In France, of course, you drive on the right. As far as driving habits are concerned, although generalisation is always a tricky business, it is fair to say that the French tend to drive faster – and are more impetuous and short-tempered – than Britons or Americans. Cross-country routes are sometimes blissfully traffic-free, though towns and cities can be intimidating at times. (A useful strategy for getting through towns is to make for the town centre, or *centre-ville*, then look out for signs indicating the way out of town in your preferred direction.)

Accidents

If no police are around, note the number of the other vehicle involved, lock your car and go with the driver of the other vehicle in search of a policeman or woman, who will make out a report in triplicate, noting all the relevant facts. Try to obtain names and addresses of witnesses. Send the report to your insurance company. If the accident is serious, it is a good idea to take photographs.

Breakdowns

If your car does not have hazard warning lights, you must carry a warning triangle, which you should place 30m (98ft) behind your car in the event of a breakdown (it is useful to have one anyway, in case the breakdown affects your lights). You must carry a set of spare headlight bulbs. On autoroutes there are emergency telephones every 2km (1^{1}/4 miles).

Car hire

To hire a car in France, drivers must have been in possession of a valid driving licence for at least one year. The minimum age is 21, though some companies insist on 25.

Car rental is easily available throughout Provence, but it is more expensive than in most other European countries. Ask at your travel agent for details of fly-drive holidays; it is usually much cheaper to book your car and flight this way than to make separate arrangements.

All the major car hire companies are represented at airports and cities in Provence – Hertz, Avis, etc. If you make your reservation before your departure, you may be able to take advantage of discounts or special rates. Take heed: the most expensive way to hire a car is to turn up at an airport desk without having made any prior arrangements. One company that offers particularly good rates, usually below those of the major operators, is **Holiday Autos** (*Holiday Autos House, Pembroke Broadway, Camberley, Surrey GU15 3XD; tel: 0870 400 4482; www.holidayautos.com*).

Chauffeur-driven cars

Every chauffeur-driven limousine company in France should have an administrative licence issued by the Ministry of Tourism (a *grande remise*) or by the Préfectures in each *département* (a *petite remise*). Around a hundred companies have the Ministry of Tourism licence. Most are affiliated to the national association of chauffeur-driven car companies:

Conversion Table		
FROM	TO	MULTIPLY BY
Inches	Centimetres	2.54
Feet	Metres	0.3048
Yards	Metres	0.9144
Miles	Kilometres	1.6090
Acres	Hectares	0.4047
Gallons	Litres	4.5460
Ounces	Grams	28.35
Pounds	Grams	453.6
Pounds	Kilograms	0.4536
Tons	Tonnes	1.0160

To convert back, for example from centimetres to inches, divide by the number in the third column.

Men's Suits

UK	36	38	40	42	44	46	48
Rest of Europe	46	48	50	52	54	56	58
USA	36	38	40	42	44	46	48

Dress Sizes

UK	8	10	12	14	16	18
France	36	38	40	42	44	46
Italy	38	40	42	44	46	48
Rest of Europe	34	36	38	40	42	44
USA	6	8	10	12	14	16

Men's Shirts

UK	14	14.5	15	15.5	16	16.5	17
Rest of Europe	36	37	38	39/40	41	42	43
USA	14	14.5	15	15.5	16	16.5	17

Men's Shoes

UK	7	7.5	8.5	9.5	10.5	11
Rest of Europe	41	42	43	44	45	46
USA	8	8.5	9.5	10.5	11.5	12

Women's Shoes

UK	4.5	5	5.5	6	6.5	7
Rest of Europe	38	38	39	39	40	41
USA	6	6.5	7	7.5	8	8.5

Chambre Syndicale Nationale des Entreprises de Remise et de Tourisme (**CSNERT**) (*7 rue Ampère, Paris 75017; tel: 01 60 17 62 98; www.csnert.fr*).

Documents

The minimum age for driving is 18. You will need to bring your driving licence, the vehicle registration document and insurance certificate. Although a Green Card – which gives you comprehensive cover and is available from your insurance company – is no longer required by law, it is strongly recommended.

Petrol

Please bear in mind that in some of Provence's remoter hill and country areas, petrol stations can be few and far between – and may well be closed altogether on Sundays. Look out for cheaper prices at larger supermarkets and hypermarkets.

Rules of the road

The *priorité à droite* (priority to the right) rule still causes confusion. Outside built-up areas, traffic flowing on the main route usually has the right of way at junctions and crossroads, which are normally signposted with a cross saying *Passage Protégé*. Within built-up areas, vehicles coming from the right – even on the most minor roads – still have priority. In practice, the French seem as confused as the rest of us over the interpretation of this arcane rule – so be extra-vigilant at junctions and, if in doubt, give way.

In recent years, the French have discovered the value of roundabouts – new ones have cropped up all over the country. Thankfully, an unambiguous rule applies: you must give way to vehicles already on the roundabout, as instructed by the sign *Vous n'avez pas la priorité* (you do not have priority).

In addition to a warning triangle and headlight bulbs, your car should have a national identity sticker and be fitted with headlight beam deflectors. Under-10s should travel in the rear seats, and the wearing of all seat belts fitted in the car is compulsory.

Speed limits

Speeds in brackets relate to adverse weather conditions (eg, heavy rain, fog, ice).
Toll motorways: 130kph/80mph (110kph/68mph).
Non-toll motorways and dual carriageways: 110kph/68mph (100kph/62mph).
Other roads: 90kph/55mph (80kph/50mph).
Towns and built-up areas: 50kph/31mph.
Please note:
Rappel means the continuation of a restriction or of a previously signposted speed limit.

The minimum speed for the outside lane of a motorway during daylight on level ground with good visibility is 80kph/50mph.

Electricity

The supply is 220 volts using continental two-pin round plugs. You will need an adaptor if you are taking your own appliances.

Embassies and consulates
Australia
4 rue Jean-Rey, 75724 Paris, Cedex 15.
Tel: 01 40 59 33 00.
Canada
35 avenue Montaigne, 75008 Paris.
Tel: 01 44 43 29 00.
Ireland
4 rue Rude, 75016 Paris.
Tel: 014417 67 00.
New Zealand
7 rue Léonard-da-Vinci, 75016 Paris.
Tel: 01 45 01 43 43.
UK
35 rue du Faubourg St-Honoré, 75383
Paris, Cedex 08. Tel: 01 44 51 31 00.
Consular section: 18 bis rue d'Anjou,
75008 Paris. Tel: 01 44 51 31 01.
Also at 24 avenue du Prado,
13006 Marseille.
Tel: 04 91 15 72 10.
USA
2 avenue Gabriel, 75382 Paris, Cedex 08.
Tel: 01 43 12 22 22. Also at Place Varian
Fry, 13086 Marseille.
Tel: 04 91 54 92 00.

Emergency telephone numbers
Ambulance *15*   **Fire** *18*
Police *17*   **Emergencies** *112*

Health
There are no mandatory vaccination
requirements, and no vaccination
recommendations other than to keep
tetanus and polio immunisation up to
date. As in every other part of the world,
AIDS is present. It is quite safe to drink
the tap water served in hotels and
restaurants, but never drink from a
tap labelled *eau non potable* (not
drinking water).

Hitchhiking
In Provence, unlike other parts of
France, hitchhiking is quite common.
The usual common-sense provisos
apply. Do not hitchhike alone, and be
wary of isolated spots. Hitchhiking is
not allowed on autoroutes.

Insurance
All EU countries have reciprocal
arrangements for reclaiming the cost of
medical services. Under an EU reciprocal
arrangement, visitors from EU countries
are entitled to medical treatment in
France, but should obtain a European
Health Insurance Card from their own
National Social Security office or from
post offices in the UK. This should be
presented to the doctor if possible before
treatment or a consultation starts.
Claiming is often a long-drawn-out
process, and you are only covered for
medical care, not for emergency
repatriation, holiday cancellation and so
on. You are strongly advised to take out a
travel insurance policy from your own
insurance company or a travel agent.

Lost property
Report loss of valuables to the police and
get a copy of the statement for making an
insurance claim. Cancel lost credit cards
and traveller's cheques immediately. A
lost passport should be reported at once
to your nearest embassy or consulate.

Maps
A wide range of maps is available (for
the best prices try some of the larger
supermarkets, which have good guide-
book/map sections). Most tourist offices
will have free town maps.

Media

In most of the major towns and cities, English-language newspapers are widely available. *Le Monde* is a respected national daily newspaper. To look up listings and local events the regional newspapers such as *La Marseillaise* or *Nice-Matin*, the leftist *Le Provençal* and the right-wing *Le Méridional* are more informative. Along the Côte d'Azur you will be able to pick up the English-language *Radio Riviera*.

Money matters

The unit of currency is the euro, which is equal to 100 cents. Bank hours vary, but typical times are Monday to Friday, 9am–noon, 2–4pm. All banks are closed on Sunday and public holidays. Some open on Saturday but close on Monday.

One of the simplest, cheapest and most secure methods of exchange is the traveller's cheque, which is accepted in hotels and larger restaurants. Usually it is advantageous to purchase cheques denominated in euros, as opposed to pounds sterling or dollars. Most banks should then give you the face value of the cheque, without deducting any further charges. Alternatively, many people use the quickest system, ATMs (cash machines), which are activated by a charge/credit card and PIN code.

Probably the most cost-effective way of all is payment by credit card; there is no transaction fee and you get the best rate of exchange. The major cards (VISA, MasterCard, etc) are widely accepted throughout Provence.

Opening hours

Apart from the big cities, France shuts down between noon and 2pm each day. In compensation, shops open very early, and many – especially the smaller stores – do not close until quite late, sometimes 8pm.

Many petrol stations and the larger supermarkets remain open throughout the day, especially in summer, as do tourist attractions and tourist offices.

Normal business hours are 8/9am–noon, and 2–6pm.

Pharmacies

These are recognised by the sign of a green cross. They give medical advice and they also sell a wide range of products (prescription and non-prescription). Many stock familiar brands of nappies (*couches*), tampons and sanitary towels (*serviettes hygiéniques*), though these can also be bought at supermarkets. Machines dispensing condoms (*préservatifs*) are often installed outside pharmacies. You will always find an open pharmacy in the area – details are posted on pharmacy doors.

Places of worship

Every town and village has a Catholic church. There are synagogues in Avignon, Carpentras and Cavaillon; Protestant churches in Nice, Toulon, Aix, Marseille and Avignon. Offer prayers at the mosques in Marseille, Nice and Toulon. Check at local tourist offices for full details.

Police

Country areas and smaller places are covered by the Gendarmerie police force

LANGUAGE

Even if you speak only a little French, the effort will be appreciated. English is widely spoken on the coast, much less so in rural Provence. But whatever your location, you will find that your attempts to speak French, however limited, will go down well.

yes	oui
no	non
please	si'l vous plaît
(any request or enquiry should be accompanied by this phrase)	
thank you	merci
good day/	bonjour
good morning	
(when addressing anyone in this way, it is common courtesy to add *monsieur* for a man, *madame* for a woman or *mademoiselle* for a girl or young woman)	
good evening	bonsoir
goodbye	au revoir
yesterday	hier
today	aujourd'hui
tomorrow	demain
the morning	le matin
afternoon	l'après-midi
the evening	le soir
man	un homme
woman	une femme
big	grand
small	petit
a lot	beaucoup
a little	un peu
open	ouvert
closed	fermé
hot	chaud
cold	froid
car	voiture
railway station	gare
bus station	gare routière
bakery	boulangerie
supermarket	supermarché
bank	banque
toilets	toilettes
post office	PTT, poste
stamps	timbres
chemist	pharmacie
hospital	hôpital

petrol	essence
airline	ligne aérienne
Do you speak English?	Parlez-vous anglais?
I do not understand	Je ne comprends pas
OK/agreed	D'accord
Where?	Où?
How much?/	Combien?
How many?	
Excuse me	Pardon
Have you a room?	Avez-vous une chambre?
Have you a room with a private bath?	Avez-vous une chambre avec bain?
How much does it cost?	Combien ça coûte?
I feel ill	Je suis malade
Have you a double room?	Avez-vous une chambre à deux lits?

0	zéro	22	vingt-deux
1	un, une	30	trente
2	deux	40	quarante
3	trois	50	cinquante
4	quatre	60	soixante
5	cinq	70	soixante-dix
6	six	80	quatre-vingts
7	sept	90	quatre-vingt-dix
8	huit	100	cent
9	neuf	200	deux cents
10	dix	300	trois cents
11	onze	1,000	mille
12	douze	2,000	deux mille
13	treize	1,000,000	un million
14	quatorze		
15	quinze	**Monday**	lundi
16	seize	**Tuesday**	mardi
17	dix-sept	**Wednesday**	mercredi
18	dix-huit	**Thursday**	jeudi
19	dix-neuf	**Friday**	vendredi
20	vingt	**Saturday**	samedi
21	vingt et un	**Sunday**	dimanche

(blue trousers, black jackets and white belts). In towns and cities, policing is provided by the Police Municipale (blue uniforms). The highway police are the Garde Mobile or Police de la Route. The emergency telephone number is *17*. In the case of very serious problems, you should contact your Consulate.

Post offices

Post offices – known as PTTs or *postes* – are usually open 9am–noon and 2–5pm, though there are many variations. You can buy stamps or telephone cards here, and some will change Euro-cheques. If you just want stamps, you can avoid queues by purchasing them at *tabacs* (tobacconists) and some hotels.

You can use post offices to receive mail through the poste restante system. Letters should be addressed with your surname printed in capital letters and underlined, followed by Poste Restante, Poste Centrale, and the postcode and name of the town.

Public transport

Along the main communication corridors in Provence – the north-south Rhône Valley and the east-west Côte d'Azur – rail and bus services are very good. Buses and trains also operate in rural and mountainous Provence, but services are patchy.

For details of up-to-date rail services and ferries from Marseille and Nice, consult the bi-monthly publication *Thomas Cook European Rail Timetable*. This is available to buy online at *www.thomascookpublishing.com* or from Thomas Cook offices (*tel: 01733 416477*).

By bus

In addition to the main rail routes, a line runs up the Durance Valley into the Alps. There are many local bus companies but not much coordination of services between them. There are also local buses run by SNCF (French Railways), which serve places on rail routes where trains do not stop (rail tickets and passes are valid on these).

The only feasible way to explore off-the-beaten-track Provence is by car, bicycle or on foot. Local tourist offices and bus stations are good sources of advice and information.

By rail

For details of unlimited-travel rail passes, contact:
In UK The Rail Shop, *French Railways, 178 Piccadilly, London W1J 9AL. Tel: 0870 241 4243 for train information; www.raileurope.com*
In USA Rail Europe, *44 South Broadway, White Plains, New York 10601. Tel: 1 888 382 7245; www.eurovacations.com*

Senior citizens

Reduced admission is available at most museums. The *Carte Vermeille*, sold at railway stations, gives reduced fares on public transport.

Student and youth travel

More than 25 per cent of visitors to France are people under the age of 26. A whole range of special services and facilities exists for this influential group.

The *Carte Jeune* (Youth Card) entitles holders – who must be under 26 – to discounts on public transport, museum admissions, entertainments, shopping and other facilities (including meals at university canteens). The card is widely available from many outlets. Details at tourist offices or post offices, or contact:

Centre d'Information et Documentation Jeunesse (National Youth Information and Documentation Centre, *101 quai Branly, 75015 Paris; tel: 08 25 09 06 30; www.cidj.com.*

For **Auberges de Jeunesse** (Youth Hostels) *see p175.*

There are special fares for under-26s on SNCF. Contact the Rail Shop for details.

Sustainable tourism

Thomas Cook is a strong advocate of ethical and fairly traded tourism and believes that the travel experience should be as good for the places visited as it is for the people who visit them. That's why we firmly support The Travel Foundation, a charity that develops solutions to help improve and protect holiday destinations, their environment, traditions and culture. To find out what you can do to make a positive difference to the places you travel to and the people who live there, please visit *www.thetravelfoundation.org.uk*

Telephones

Coin-operated phone booths are no longer common and the *télécarte* phone card has taken over. Buy one in a post office or *tabac* (tobacconists). The cards are much cheaper than a hotel call and simple to use.

Many phones now accept credit cards too. Cheap rates operate after 8pm and all day Sunday. French telephone numbers have ten digits, the first two indicate the region: Paris and the Ile de France *01*, the northwest *02*, the northeast *03*, the southeast including Corsica *04*, the southwest *05*. When phoning France from abroad do not include the initial zero of the French number.

To make an international call from France, dial *00*, then the country code: **Australia** *61*, **Canada** *1*, **Ireland** *353*, **New Zealand** *64*, **UK** *44*, **USA** *1*. For international directory enquiries dial *3212*.

Time

France observes Central European Time. For the UK and Ireland, France is one hour ahead of Greenwich Mean Time from late September to late March, and two hours ahead for the rest of the year. France is six to nine hours ahead of the USA, five to nine hours ahead of Canada, seven to nine hours behind Australia and 11 hours behind New Zealand.

Tipping

In restaurants and cafés, service is generally included in the bill. If not, leave an extra 10–15 per cent. Taxi drivers should be tipped 10–15 per cent of the amount on the meter. In hotels, tip porters €1–2 for every item of baggage and chambermaids about €2 a day. Cloakroom attendants in theatres and restaurants should be tipped about €1 per item, toilet attendants 50c, and guides at museums and historic monuments about €1. A 10 per cent tip should be given to hairdressers.

Toilets

There are public toilets at stations, in public buildings and in stores. In the smaller towns, there may be just one toilet to be shared by both men (*hommes* or *messieurs*) and women (*dames*).

Tourist offices

For information on Provence, contact your local French Government Tourist Office or check *www.franceguide.com*

Australia
Level 13, 25 Bligh Street, Sydney, NSW 2000. Tel: 292 315 244.
Canada
Headquarters *1981 Avenue McGill College, Suite 490, Montréal, QUE H3A 2W9. Tel: (514) 288 2026.*
Ireland
35 Lower Abbey Street, Dublin 1. Tel: 1560 235 235.
UK
The French Travel Centre, 178 Piccadilly, London W1J 9AL. Tel: 09068 244123.
USA
Headquarters *444 Madison Avenue, 10022 New York. Tel: 1514 288 1904.*
Midwest *205 Michigan Avenue, Chicago, Illinois 60611. Tel: 514 288 1904.*
West Coast *9454 Wilshire Boulevard, Beverly Hills, Los Angeles, CA 90212. Tel: 514 288 1904.*

Although the first point of contact is your country's French Tourist Office, it is often worth getting in touch directly with the region for the most up-to-date literature, or surf their websites:
Comité Régional de Tourisme
Provence-Alpes-Côte d'Azur, *BP4621–F13567, Marseille. Tel: 04 91 56 47 00; www.decouverte-paca.fr*
You could also try these websites:
www.alpes-haute-provence.com;
www.alpes-maritimes.net;
www.visitprovence.com; www.hautes-alpes.net; www.tourismevar.com;
www.provenceguide.com

When in France, use the local network of tourist information offices – the Office de Tourisme or Syndicat d'Initiative – located in most towns and many villages. In addition to providing details of local events, walks, activities, etc, some will change money and help with accommodation for a small fee.

Travellers with disabilities

In recent times, more efforts have been made to welcome travellers with disabilities. In addition to providing better on-the-ground facilities, individual resorts and areas produce publications that give information on accommodation, transport, recreational activities, access to historic monuments, museums, theatres, etc.

For more information, contact:
Association des Paralysés *Délégation de Paris, 13 Place de Rungis, 75013 Paris. Tel: 01 53 80 92 97; www.apf.asso.fr*
Centre Technique National d'Etudes et Recherches sur le Handicap *236 bis rue de Tolbaic, Paris 75013. Tel: 01 45 65 59 00.*

In Britain, contact: **Maison de la France** *178 Piccadilly, London W1J 9AL. Tel: 090 6824 4123; www.franceguide.com.* A factsheet on France is available from the **Holiday Care Service**, *The Hawkins Suite, Enham Place, Enham Alamein, Andover SP11 6JS. Tel: 0845 124 9971; www.holidaycare.org.uk.* The *AA Guide for the Disabled Traveller* is another helpful publication.

ACKNOWLEDGEMENTS
Thomas Cook Publishing wishes to thank the following libraries and associations for their assistance in the preparation of this book.

FIONA NICHOLS 1, 3, 15, 18, 21, 22a, 26a, 30b, 32, 41b, 48, 51, 52, 56, 57a, 58, 61, 66, 70b, 80, 81, 90a, 90b, 113, 131, 132, 135a 139a, 141, 144, 152a, 152b, 153, 154, 159, 160, 162, 165, 168a, 168b, 169, 175, 179, 183, 189
MARY EVANS PICTURE LIBRARY 30a, 105, 117
PICTURES COLOUR LIBRARY 19, 97
RONALD GRANT ARCHIVES 96, 104a

The remaining pictures are held in the AA PHOTO LIBRARY and were taken by ADRIAN BAKER, with the exception of pages 5, 10, 11, 13, 31a, 31b, 34, 35, 37, 42a, 42b, 44b, 45, 53, 57b, 59, 60a, 63, 64, 70a, 78b, 85b, 92, 94, 95, 106b, 115, 118a, 119, 130a, 130-131, 133, 134, 135b, 146c, 156, 161a, 161b, 170a, 170b, 172 which were taken by RICK STRANGE; pages 17, 93, 110, 111, 118b, 120, 122, 124a, 126a, 126b, 138 which were taken by ROB MOSS; pages 65, 76, 86 which were taken by BARRIE SMITH; and page 47 which was taken by T OLIVER.

Index: MARIE LORIMER

Proofreading: JAN McCANN FOR CAMBRIDGE PUBLISHING MANAGEMENT LIMITED

Send your thoughts to
books@thomascook.com

We're committed to providing the very best up-to-date information in our travel guides and constantly strive to make them as useful as they can be. You can help us to improve future editions by letting us have your feedback. If you've made a wonderful discovery on your travels that we don't already feature, if you'd like to inform us about recent changes to anything that we do include, or if you simply want to let us know your thoughts about this guidebook and how we can make it even better – we'd love to hear from you.

Send us ideas, discoveries and recommendations today and then look out for your valuable input in the next edition of this title. And, as an extra 'thank you' from Thomas Cook Publishing, you'll be automatically entered into our exciting monthly prize draw.

Emails to the above address, or letters to Travellers Project Editor, Thomas Cook Publishing, PO Box 227, Unit 18, Coningsby Road, Peterborough PE3 8SB, UK.

Please don't forget to let us know which title your feedback refers to!